BIG TRUTH LIT

WHAT THE BIBLE SAYS ABOUT THE FUTURE

Colin Eakin

GBF Press
Cupertino, California

WHAT THE BIBLE SAYS ABOUT THE FUTURE

What the Bible Says About the Future is volume 16 in the Big Truth little books® series.

General Editor: Cliff McManis
Series Editor: Derek Brown
Associate Editors: J. R. Cuevas, Breanna Paniagua, Jasmine Patton
Proofreader: Sergio Gonzalez
Cover Design: Oluwasanya Awe

Dedicated to Pastor John MacArthur,
Faithful expositor of God's plan for the future

"After this I looked, and behold,
A door standing open in heaven!
And the first voice,
which I had heard speaking to me
like a trumpet, said,
'Come up here, and I will show you
what must take place after this.'"

The Revelation of Jesus Christ, 4:1

CONTENTS

SERIES PREFACE

Our mission with the *BIG TRUTH little books*® series is to provide edifying, accessible literature for Christian readers from all walks of life. We understand that it is often difficult to find time to read good books. But we also understand that reading is a valuable means of spiritual growth. The answer? Get some really big truth into some little books. These books may be small, but each is full of Scripture, theological reflection, and pastoral insight. Our hope is that Christians young and old will benefit from these books as they grow in their knowledge of Christ through His Word.

Cliff McManis, General Editor
Derek Brown, Series Editor

FOREWORD

For a number of years, it has been my privilege and pleasure to partner with Pastor Derek Brown in teaching the Stanford student group, Grace Campus Ministries. This past year's (2018-2019) theme was "Christian Doctrine," culminating in a two-week survey of biblical eschatology, or what the Bible says about the future. Based upon enthusiastic student response, the idea arose to summarize the material into a format to fit the GBF Press's BIG TRUTH little book series, providing a "bite size" overview of what the Bible has to say about the future for wider distribution.

The doctrine of the future of this world is not an optional or trivial one for Christians, nor is it one where any one of a number of possible theories will suffice. But how is one to know which interpretive scheme is correct? How can one be sure of what the Bible really says about the future and how this world will end?

Here I find a story Pastor John MacArthur tells in his teaching ministry most helpful. Shortly after the breakup of the Soviet Union, Pastor MacArthur agreed to fly the thirty hours to Kazakhstan to teach at a weeklong conference with 1,600 pastors. Toward the end of the week, he was asked, "When are you going to get to the 'good part?'"

"What's the 'good part?'" he inquired.

"We want to know what happens in the end," they replied. These men had been pastoring congregations subjected to harsh conditions and persecution for many years. Their lives and the lives of those to whom they ministered were barren of the many worldly pleasures that wealth and freedom provide. These men wanted to know what the future held, where their hopes were set. They wanted to know about the end of this world and the glory of the next.

So MacArthur took that Friday and for eight hours covered as many points on biblical eschatology as he could, not knowing what perspective these pastors held. When he had finished, the leaders sat down with him and said, "You believe exactly the way we do."

He was astonished. "Are you kidding?" he marveled. "You mean you believe everything exactly the way I've just taught?"

"Yes," they averred. "That's exactly what we believe."

MacArthur contends the reason for this eschatological alignment is because they were all reading the same Bible. In other words, one has to be exposed to outside influences to unlearn what Scripture clearly teaches on the doctrine of the future. These pastors had not been subjected to the revisionist proposals of misguided seminaries, commentaries and other sources of error, designed to draw into question the clarity of Scripture. All they had was the Bible, and they believed it as it was plainly written.

That is the task for all of us—to believe what the Bible says, plainly and clearly. On the pages that follow, the challenge is to allow the Word of God to speak for itself. Let the words and phrases mean exactly what they appear to be saying. As you do, you too will understand the future as God intends.

To the glory of God forever.

Colin Eakin
Creekside Bible Church
July, 2019

INTRODUCTION

"Doesn't the Bible say something about the future?"

Has that thought ever crossed your mind? The Bible does indeed say *much* about the future. In fact, the Bible is the definitive guide to the purpose of this world and where it is headed. The Bible is more reliable in what it says about the future than what a history book might tell you of the past or a newspaper (or website) might tell you about the present. How is that possible? Because this is God's world, and the Bible is God's Word. So if we want to know the purpose and end of God's world, we must know what God has said about it in His Word.

God wrote His Word as the story of His creation, with a beginning, middle and an ending. The Bible's story of this world thus records its past, describes its present, and tells of its future. And running throughout this story at every bend and turn is a singular, overarching theme—*the glory of God.* Everything God wrote in His Word is meant to portray and extol His glory. In **Isaiah 40:5**, the prophet writes what God has determined: "**the glory of the LORD shall be revealed**...." The purpose of creation is to reveal and magnify the glory of God.

What is the glory of God? It is the comprehensive summation of all God's qualities, coalesced together in magnificent brilliance. The glory of God includes His holiness, love, peace, and joy, as well as His patience, grace, mercy and forgiveness. It even includes His wrath against sin and determination to judge all wrongdoing. The Bible declares that God created the world to put His glory on display, so that His entire creation might glorify Him (**Ps 50:15; Isa 48:11**).

One particular feature of God's glory is His sovereignty. This means God controls every detail of His creation. **Ephesians 1:11** says God **"works all things according to the counsel of His will."** The operative phrase is **"all things."** Nothing is outside of God's attention and control, at all times and in all places. **Isaiah 46:10** says God is able to declare, **"the end from the beginning, and from ancient times things not yet done, saying, 'My counsel shall stand, and I will accomplish all My purpose.'"** This last verse shows that God is not only sovereign, but providential as well. Providence is sovereignty with a plan, and God is providentially overseeing all things right down to their divinely appointed end (**Ps 115:3**).

This last idea—God's planned end for all things within His creation—is the topic of this book. The study of the future is known as *eschatology*, and it is our task to study what God has said about it. Because of an unwarranted belief that matters of eschatology are obscure, divisive, or unimportant, many churches fail to give any systematic teaching on the topic. When not considered strictly *verboten*, matters of eschatology are often treated without any Scriptural precision or confidence, and are usually relegated to a vague and rarely spoken understanding that Jesus is somehow, some way, returning to right the world. As for all the prophecies in the Old and New Testaments describing in great detail God's plan for how the world will end, and what the eternal future will bring? They are generally dismissed as unintelligible allegories, and are therefore deemed contentious and unimportant.

But that is not how God wants His followers to treat His Word. Jesus quotes **Deuteronomy 8:3** when He proclaims, **"Man shall not live by bread alone, but by *every word that comes from the mouth of God*"** (**Matt 4:4**; italics added), and that includes His prophetic utterances. Hebrews categorizes matters of the **"resurrection of the dead"** and **"eternal judgment"** as **"elementary doctrine"** (**Heb 6:2**). Paul agreed. Although he was only there for a very short period, Paul taught the church in Thessalonica so much eschatology that Paul considered it fully instructed in both the coming of the Antichrist (**2 Thess 2:5**) and the subsequent Second Coming of Christ (**1 Thess 5:1-2**). And Revelation, which describes the future in more detail than any other book, is the only book of the Bible that both begins and ends with a blessing for all who read and understand it (**1:3; 22:7**). God wrote His Word so that it might be comprehended and thereby edify its readers, and that includes all He has written about the future.

Why Study the Future?

This then is the first of five biblical reasons[1] why God instructs the readers of His Word to study and understand its prophecies: that such understanding might *bless* those who seek to know what God says will take place. A second reason to study what God has said about the future is that it might bring about *repentance*—a vital criterion for salvation. Paul says to the Athenians at Mars Hill, **"The times of ignorance God overlooked, but now He commands all people everywhere to *repent*, because He has fixed a day on which He will judge the world in righteousness by a Man whom He has appointed; and of this He has given assurance to all by raising Him from the dead"** (**Acts 17:30-31**; emphasis added). Knowledge that Jesus Christ is returning as the world's righteous judge is meant to generate repentance among all those enlightened to this reality.

A third reason to read and understand prophetic texts of Scripture is the *purity* that such an endeavor brings. John wrote, **"Beloved, we are God's children** now, and what we will be has not yet appeared; but we know that when He appears, we shall be like him because we shall see Him like He is. And everyone who thus hopes in Him *purifies* himself as He is pure" (1 John 3:2-3; emphasis added). Jesus offered a similar insight when He instructed His apostles, **"But know this, that if the master of the house had known in what part of the night the thief was coming, he would have stayed awake and would not have let his house be broken into"** (**Matt 24:43**). What Jesus and John are stating is axiomatic: if you know Christ might return at any time, you will be more likely to strive for purity in your life's pursuits.

Fourth, comprehension of biblical prophecy brings *comfort and reassurance*. In **1 Thessalonians 4:16-17**, Paul unveils God's plan for the rapture of the Church: **"For the Lord Himself will descend from heaven with a cry of command, with the voice of the archangel, and with the sound of the trumpet of God. And the dead in Christ will rise first. Then we who are alive, who are left, will be caught up together with Him in the clouds to meet the Lord in the air, and so we will always be with the Lord."** And what is his point in revealing this mystery? **Verse 18: "Therefore, encourage one another with these words."** Paul wants believers to know the future so that they might hearten and reassure fellow believers regarding what is shortly to take place.

The fifth reason to study and understand biblical prophecy is *simply because God wrote about it!* God's writing is never trivial or superfluous (**Prov 30:5; 2 Tim 3:16**). If it matters to God to include an ending to His story, it should matter to His followers to comprehend that ending. In fact, Jesus teaches that the world is accountable for everything God has written in His Word (**Luke 16:29; John 12:48**), and this includes His revelation about the future.

How to Study the Future

Having established *why* Christians should study what God says about the future, the next logical question is *how?* How does one assimilate all the Old and New Testament prophetic texts intelligibly and with confidence? Answer: *literally*. In general, readers of prophecy should process such information just as they do other portions of Scripture, anticipating that the information is being presented in a straightforward, indicative manner and is subject to a "plain-meaning" interpretation, or *hermeneutic*.

How do we know a literal hermeneutic is a valid way to study biblical prophecy? *We look to the Bible.* Did you know that many biblical prophecies were actually fulfilled within the scope of its events? In other words, both the prophecy and its fulfillment are recorded within the time course of Scripture,[2] most notably surrounding the promise of the Messiah. These are extraordinarily valuable examples, for they provide the critical validation of a literal hermeneutic for interpretation of Scriptural prophecy.

Specifically, there are approximately 333 prophecies in Scripture about the coming of the Messiah, of which approximately 111 were fulfilled—*literally*—with His first coming.[3] These include such well-known predictions that He would be born in Bethlehem (**Micah 5:2**), of the tribe of Judah (**Gen 49:10**), to a virgin, and that He would be called "Immanuel" (**Isa 7:14**). The prophecies further declare the Messiah would be rejected by His people (**Isa 53:3**) and betrayed by His friend (**Ps 41:9**), that He would die upon a cross (**Num 21:9; John 3:14**) and subsequently rise to life again (**Ps 16:10**). Christians rejoice at the literal fulfillment of these and other prophecies regarding the first coming of Christ. These corroborated prophecies therefore represent an authenticated framework for the literal interpretation of the many yet-unfulfilled prophecies regarding Christ's Second Coming. To interpret prophecies of Christ's first arrival literally and then insist upon a different hermeneutic with regard to prophecies of His Second Coming is illegitimate.

What about the interpretation of eschatological passages within the Bible itself? Does Scripture provide any examples where biblical persons use a literal hermeneutic for prophetic interpretation? Indeed it does, and from a particularly devout and approved man of God (**Ezek 14:14; 28:3; Dan 9:23**).

The year is around 538 B.C. The people of Judah, what remained of God's chosen people, had been exiled from their land into captivity in Babylon in three deportations, beginning around 605 B.C. and culminating in 586 B.C. All of this was predicted by the prophet Jeremiah, who wrote, **"This whole land shall become a ruin and a waste, and these nations shall serve the king of Babylon seventy years. Then after seventy years are completed, I will punish the king of Babylon and that nation, the land of the Chaldeans, for their iniquity, declares the LORD, making the land an everlasting waste"** (Jer 25:11-12). In another passage, he adds, **"For thus says the LORD: When seventy years are completed for Babylon, I will visit you, and I will fulfill to you My promise and bring you back into this place"** (Jer 29:10).

The prophet Daniel, then a youth, was among those taken captive to Babylon in the first deportation. Nevertheless, through God's empowerment and blessing, he rose to become the governor of the entire kingdom of Babylon. And when the Medes and Persians conquered the Babylonians in 539 B.C., Daniel maintained his position through his divinely granted wisdom and competence. But even in his position of authority, Daniel never lost the desire to see his people, the Jews, return to their Promised Land. And so it was that, late in his life, Daniel remembered the prophecies of Jeremiah regarding the coming captivity of his people, and when their exile would end. As he contemplates this imminent date, Daniel explains, **"I, Daniel, perceived in the books the number of years that, according to the Word of the LORD to Jeremiah the prophet, must pass before the end of the desolations of Jerusalem, namely, seventy years"** (Dan 9:2).

In other words, Daniel interpreted Scriptural prophecy in a literal manner. He read where Jeremiah wrote "seventy years" and believed it meant "seventy years." *Seventy literal years.* Daniel did not try to spiritualize or allegorize the text. He did not assume that "seventy years" represented some abstract concept subject to multiple interpretations. He interpreted "seventy years" to mean precisely what we would expect it to mean. And in fact, the prophecy came to pass exactly as it was written. Seventy years from the captivity of Judah to Babylon, Cyrus, the king of Persia decreed that the Israelites could return to their land (**Ezra 1:1-4**). As with all His prophecies, what God wrote through the hand of Jeremiah came about exactly as foretold. Here, then, is further precedent for the literal interpretation of prophetic texts.

Amazingly, the Bible even gives an example where failure to interpret prophecy in a literal manner brought catastrophe. Upon the conquest of Jericho (c. 1400 B.C.), Joshua, the leader of the people of Israel, pronounced a prophetic oath upon its ruins, saying,

"Cursed before the LORD be the man who rises up and rebuilds this city, Jericho." He then specifies the penalty that will ensue: **"At the cost of his firstborn shall he lay its foundation, and at the cost of his youngest son shall he set up its gates"** (Josh 6:26). For five hundred years, that prophecy lingered over the desolation of Jericho, until the reign of the wicked King Ahab (c. 875-853 B.C.), when Hiel of Bethel set about to do what Joshua had said should not be done. The text does not say if Hiel was either unaware of or unconcerned by Joshua's historic curse—all we know is that it did not dissuade him from his task. Sadly, Hiel's effort in Jericho's urban revival came at huge personal cost: he lost his oldest son, Abiram, when he laid the new foundation for Jericho, and then lost his youngest son, Segub, when he set up its gates (1 Kings 16:34). The prophecy was fulfilled *literally*, in perfect accord with what Joshua had stated under the inspiration of the Holy Spirit. The lesson? Not only will using a literal hermeneutic for eschatological interpretation bless its reader, failure to handle such portions of Scripture in this manner can bring personal disaster and heartbreaking tragedy.

So that is the *why* and the *how* of prophetic interpretation. With this established, we are now able to embark upon a journey into what the Bible says about the future. But before we look forward to what the future holds, we must look back in time, *to the time before there was time*, to see where things are headed.

1

BEFORE TIME BEGAN

When we look to the future as God has written it, we necessarily encounter a critical concept: *time*. There was no time before God created it. Prior to this, God existed forever in the eternal past as the Trinity, consisting of the Father, the Son (Jesus), and the Holy Spirit. Because God is the Creator of time, He exists above and beyond its boundaries and limitations. Because God transcends and governs time and all that occurs within it, His pronouncements about time are certain. In other words, when God says something happened in the past or will happen in the future, it is a fact.

God's first reference to time in His Word occurs in its first sentence, **Genesis 1:1: "In the beginning, God created the heavens and the earth."** This is when the universal clock started ticking, at the moment of creation. But this is *not* the earliest revelation we have of this world and God's purpose for it. The Bible actually reveals the thoughts and experiences of God *prior to the beginning of time*, and this is where we must go to comprehend God's design for the future—a design that centers around a Person, a plan, a prerogative and a proclamation.

To know the *Person* around whom all history is oriented, and especially regarding God's design for the future, we look to the Gospel of John, Chapter 17. Here, this central Person—God the Son, Jesus Christ—unveils His relationship with God the Father as nowhere else in Scripture, a relationship that centers around their shared glory. As presented in the Introduction, the revelation of the glory of God is the theme of all Scripture. And in **verse 5**, Jesus makes an interesting request to His Father regarding that divine glory, as He prays, **"And now, Father, glorify Me in your own presence with the glory I had with you before the world existed."** Jesus is saying in the eternal past, He enjoyed a glorious existence with His Father, one He now desired to be fully showcased. Then in **verse 24**, Jesus continues, **"Father, I desire they also, whom You have given Me, may be with Me where I am, to see My glory that you have given Me, because you loved Me before the foundation of the world."**

What is this glory God the Son was given by God the Father before time began, a glory Jesus desires to be fully displayed? And who are the ones given to the Son by the Father? The Bible reveals that the glory

God the Father is bequeathing to His Son centers on a kingdom, given to the Son by the Father. The prophet Daniel describes it as follows:

> **I saw in the night visions, and behold, with the clouds of heaven there came one like a son of man** [i.e. God the Son, Jesus Christ][1]**, and He came to the Ancient of Days** [i.e. God the Father] **and was presented before Him. And to Him was given dominion and glory and a kingdom, that all peoples, nations, and languages should serve Him; His dominion is an everlasting dominion, which shall not pass away, and His kingdom one that shall not be destroyed (7:13-14).**

In other words, before time began, God the Father designed to give His Son a kingdom, whose citizens would represent a cross-section of all peoples, nations and languages, forever marveling at the Son's glory and worshipping Him for it. This coming kingdom, then, is where everything with regard to the future is aiming. If you ever become confused in your study of eschatology, you can reorient yourself by recalling this fundamental truth: all things are headed toward the kingdom God the Father has determined to give to His Son, Jesus Christ.

What about the makeup of the kingdom? Who are to be its citizens, whom Jesus describes as given to the Son by the Father, and how do they become eligible? To answer this, let us return to John 17 and look at God the Father's *plan* for delivering this kingdom to His Son. The chapter begins with Christ's statement to His Father that, **"the hour has come"** (**v. 17:1b; cf. 12:23**). What hour? We get a clue from **1 Peter 1:20**, where it says of Christ: ***"He was foreknown before the foundation of the world** but was made manifest in the last times for the sake of you* [believers]" (emphasis added). Foreknown as what? **Verses 18-19** give the answer, when it says of these believers, **"... you were ransomed from the futile ways inherited from your forefathers, not with perishable things such as silver and gold, but with the precious blood of Christ, like that of a lamb without blemish or spot."**

What Peter is saying is before the foundation of the world, God the Father planned to send His Son, Jesus Christ, as the perfect Lamb of God who would ransom sinners from their sin. This is what **Hebrews 13:20** refers to as the **"eternal covenant"** between God the Father and His Son. The implication of this covenant from the eternal past is profound: sin and its only sufficient atonement via the shedding of blood (**Lev 17:11; Heb 9:22**) were both anticipated before the foundation of the world. In other words, God's plan that Christ would die for sinners was established before any sinner ever existed! It is for this reason that the Apostle Paul writes, **"[God] saved us and called us to a holy calling, not because of our works but because of His own purpose and grace, which He gave us in Christ Jesus *before the ages began*"** (**2 Tim 1:9**; emphasis added).

God the Father thus determined before time began that He would save sinners and call sinners by His own grace and for His own purpose. This purpose, we now know, is for those who are redeemed by Christ to forever worship Him in His kingdom for His sacrifice in suffering the just punishment for sin on their behalf (**Lam 3:1; Rev 5:9-11**). The hour of which Jesus spoke in **John 17:1** was the hour God the Father had determined before time began would be the pinnacle of all history, when His Son would endure the Father's wrath in judgment against every sin of all who would ever repent and believe in the Son's substitutionary sacrifice, and so satisfy the divine condition for atonement (cf. **Isa 54:4-6; 9-11; 1 John 2:2; 4:10**). Scripture says this is the highest form love has ever taken (**John 15:13; Rom 5:6, 8-10**), and since love is preeminent among the holy virtues of God (**1 Cor 13:13**), Christ's suffering in obedience to His Father's will is the most glorious act of all time. Knowing all this was imminent, Jesus' desire at the Last Supper prior to His crucifixion was for the Father to share in the glory He was about to display, which is why He proclaims, **"Now is the Son of Man** glorified, and God is glorified in Him. If God is glorified in Him, God will also glorify Him in Himself, and glorify Him at once" (John 13:31-32).

There is something more to emphasize about those giving tribute to Christ for His glory in His kingdom to come: each and every one of the kingdom's citizens was chosen by God the Father individually and by name in eternity past (**John 6:37, 44; 1 Cor 1:26-31**). Note how Paul unveils this truth in his second letter to the Thessalonians (NKJV): **"But we are bound to give thanks to God always for you, brethren beloved by the Lord, *because God from the beginning chose you for salvation* through sanctification by the Spirit and belief in the truth, to which He called you by our gospel, for the obtaining of the glory of our Lord Jesus Christ"** (**2 Thess 2:13-14**; emphasis added). To the Ephesians, Paul explains that God the Father, **"...*chose us in Him before the foundation of the world,* that we should be holy and blameless before Him. In love He predestined us for adoption to Himself as sons through Jesus Christ, *according to the purpose of His will,* to the praise of his glorious grace, with which he has blessed us in the Beloved"** (**1:4-5**; emphasis added). In other words, God chose a portion of humanity before time began—the elect of God—to be saved from their sin by His Son, all according to His own purpose and plan that His Son might be eternally glorified. Paul states

22

his entire ministry is, **"...for the sake of the *elect*, that they also may obtain the salvation that is in Christ Jesus with eternal glory"** (2 Tim 2:10; emphasis added).

This is a stunning revelation: every person who comes to Christ was chosen by the Father prior to His creation of the world (**John 6:37, 44, 65**). In other words, the future kingdom participants were determined by the *prerogative* of God before time began. They were individually selected and their names were written down in the Lamb's Book of Life before any of them ever came into being (**Rev 13:8; 17:8**), all for the purpose of exalting the Son's glory forever. Does that sound unfair to you, that God would choose some and not others for the kingdom He planned to give to His Son? That's understandable, because it's a human inclination, spawning from the human mind. But you must remember the human mind has been corrupted by sin, and cannot be trusted to know what is truly fair or right in this world (**Eph 4:17-18; Titus 1:15**). Prior to its regeneration by Christ, the human mind is incapable of understanding the true justice of God (**Rom 8:7-8**). Not only that, the events of this world are not arranged around what humans think is right or best, but around what God has determined will portray His glory most magnificently. Notice again God's rationale for His sovereign election of sinners, that they might be **"to the praise of *His* glorious grace...."** (**Eph 1:5;** emphasis added). The salvation of sinners, as with all things, is ultimately designed to enhance the glory of God.

How was all this to be known? How were humans ever to understand God's sovereign, eternal plan, demanding repentance from sin and belief in the Savior's sacrifice to save? Here we come to God's *proclamation*, the Word of God, also foreknown before time began. Paul writes to the church in Corinth, **"...we impart a secret and hidden wisdom of God, which God decreed *before the ages* for our glory"** (**1 Cor 2:7**; emphasis added). What is this **"secret and hidden wisdom"** which God planned before He made the world? His *holy Word*, and in particular the *gospel*, **"the power of God for salvation to everyone who believes"** (**Rom 1:16**). Of this gospel, Paul declares he was **"made a minister according to the gift of God's grace...to bring to light for everyone what is *the plan of the mystery hidden for ages in God* who created all things, so that through the church the manifold wisdom of God might now be made known to the rulers and authorities in the heavenly places"** (**Eph 3:7, 9-10**; emphasis added). Paul is saying that God's plan for the purpose and future of the world was not only known by Him, but was actually established in His Word prior to the existence of time. And it is this Word, and this Word only, to which we must turn if we are to understand the future God has planned for the world.

What have we learned in this chapter? The Triune God experienced a Trinitarian glory between its Persons from eternity past. Out of this glorious existence, God the Father determined before the foundation of the world to glorify His Son by giving Him a kingdom, made up of a wide cross-section of redeemed sinners. Of His own prerogative, He chose these sinners individually for the purpose of glorifying His Son, who would pay the price of their atonement and so rescue them from their deserved damnation. As we have seen, the Bible is clear this was all transpiring within the mind of God before time began, before any creation had occurred.

A kingdom for Christ is coming in the future, planned from eternity past and made up of individuals elected by God, all for the praise of His glory. But how is this to come about? Who are these "chosen people?" And how is this kingdom to be made manifest? We'll answer these questions in the next chapter.

2

ISRAEL: KEY TO THE FUTURE

Readers of the Bible will soon encounter a term that is ubiquitous throughout Scripture: *Israel*. God declares He is **"the King of Israel, and His Redeemer"** (Isa **44:6**). He says of Israel, **"I formed you; you are My servant O Israel, you will not be forgotten by Me"** (**44:21**). He further says of Israel that He has, **"blotted out your transgressions like a cloud, and your sins like a mist,"** and that the heavens and earth should rejoice. Why? **"For the LORD has redeemed Jacob, and will be glorified in Israel"** (**44:22-23**). Finally, God has promised, **"I will bring near My righteousness; it is not far off, and my salvation will not delay; I will put salvation in Zion, for Israel My glory"** (**46:13**).

Clearly, Israel is very important to God. The passages above show that Israel was formed by God, has been redeemed by God, will not be forgotten by God, and ultimately will glorify God. God's purpose for Israel dominates the narrative of the Old Testament and culminates in the New Testament. So to whom or what does this term Israel refer? Because of a widespread and deep-seated resistance to the literal interpretation of Scripture, many surmise that when God speaks of Israel, He means something other than the ethnic people of Jewish descent. One popular view contends that ethnic "Israel" has been replaced by "the Church." So the Church is called the "New Israel" and thus supplants Old Testament Jews and promises made to them, because of their national rejection of the Messiah. This aberrant view of Israel and the Church is called *replacement theology*, in that some other group "replaces" ethnic Israel when the Bible refers to "Israel."

The only way to arrive at this conclusion is to do away with the normal rules of biblical interpretation. Inevitably, those who aim to substitute some group other than ethnic Israel when the Bible says "Israel" must spiritualize or allegorize the text away from its literal intent. On what biblical license this is done is unclear, for you will not find any textual authorization to interpret "Israel" as any entity other than the race of Jewish descendants. Put another way, whenever the Bible references Israel, it is always and only referencing that people known as the Jews, ethnically descended from Abraham, Isaac, and Jacob (later Israel).

Why is this so important to clarify? Because the basis for understanding end times lies in understanding God's covenantal promises to His chosen people, Israel. In other words, *the cornerstone of all eschatology is Israel.* Only with a proper understanding of God's purpose and plan for Israel does one have the foundation for understanding all future prophecy in the Word of God. Here, MacArthur presents a helpful continuum to aid our understanding:

1) You will get your eschatology right when you get Israel right;

2) You will get Israel right when you get the Old Testament covenants right;

3) You will get the Old Testament covenants right when you get the interpretation of Scripture right; and,

4) You will get the interpretation of Scripture right when you are faithful to its valid rules of interpretation, which means accepting the plain meaning of Scripture as you read it.

According to such a literal interpretation, what are the covenantal promises God has given to Israel? There are five main ones relative to the subject at hand. In the order that God gave them, they include the Abrahamic, Mosaic, Palestinian, Davidic and the New

Covenant. All the covenants to Israel have some common features including the following: (1) they are all initiated by God and contingent upon His grace; (2) they were given in a time of crisis or transition; (3) no covenant nullifies a previous one; (4) each covenant promised blessings for obedience and curses for disobedience; (5) all the covenants find their ultimate fulfillment and significance in Christ.[1] A few highlights of each are in order. The first, the *Abrahamic Covenant*, was issued when God called Abram out of Ur and sent Him to the Promised Land of Canaan. Of His own sovereign prerogative and purpose, God blessed Abram (later Abraham), saying, **"...I will make of you a great nation, and I will bless you and make your name great, so that you will be a blessing. I will bless those who bless you, and him who dishonors you I will curse, and in you all the families of the earth shall be blessed"** (Gen 12:2-3). What specifics did this blessing entail? In a nutshell, God would make Abram a nation; and every nation requires three essentials: people, property and politics; or laity, land and laws. The promise of a nation with descendants too numerous to count, i.e. laity (**Gen 13:16; 17:4-6; 22:17**); land with territorial boundaries known even to this day (**13:14-15; 15:18-21; 17:8**); and, most critically, the coming of a victorious Offspring, a Leader with laws (**22:17-18**). How long was this blessing to be in effect? *Forever* (cf. **Gen 13:15; Luke 1:55**). God repeatedly describes His unilateral, unconditional, and often-repeated blessings to Abraham as **"everlasting"** (**Gen 13, 17:7-8, 19**). The Apostle Paul declares them **"irrevocable"** (**Rom 11:29**).

Nearly a millennium later, God expands His promises of the Abrahamic Covenant with the *Davidic Covenant.* In **2 Samuel 7:12**, God (again, as with Abraham, unilaterally and unconditionally) declares to King David, **"When your days are fulfilled and you lie down with your fathers, I will raise up your Offspring after you, Who shall come from your body, and I will establish His kingdom."** He continues in **verse 16**: **"And your house, and your kingdom shall be made sure forever before Me. Your throne shall be established forever."** The Davidic promise is reiterated in **Psalm 89**: **"Once for all I have sworn by My holiness; I will not lie to David. His Offspring shall endure forever, and his throne as long as the sun before Me"** (**89:35-36**). So what has God promised to Israel through His covenant with David? An eternal kingdom, to be ruled by a forever King, the Offspring of David.

But in between the Abrahamic and Davidic Covenants lies the Mosaic Covenant. God used the Mosaic Covenant to prepare the people for the fulfillment of the previous covenants in addition to the yet-to-come New Covenant. The Ten Commandments, the hundreds of civil and legal ordinances, the sacrifices, the feast days, the

Tabernacle and all its accouterments within the Mosaic Covenant were all pictures, symbols and types used by God to tutor and prepare Israel, to show them their need for a Savior by illustrating concretely God's holiness and man's sinfulness and helplessness. The Mosaic Law or Covenant was a complement to the Abrahamic Covenant, developing and even furthering specific components of it that would lead to the greater, or "better" New Covenant (**Heb 7:22; cf. Lev 26**). Paul makes it clear when contrasting the Abrahamic Covenant with the Mosaic Covenant: **"Why the Law then? It was added because of transgressions, having been ordained through angels by the agency of a mediator, until the seed** [Messiah] **would come to whom the promise had been made"** (**Gal 3:19**). Further he says the Mosaic Covenant **"has become our tutor to lead us to Christ"** (**3:24**). All the covenants following the Abrahamic were further developments of its particular features. This is the nature of progressive revelation (**Rom 9:4**).

Because the Bible records Israel's failure to comply with the Mosaic Law's demands repeatedly and miserably, it might be concluded that God's other promises through Abraham and David are then nullified. Is this true? Note how Paul decisively refutes this idea in **Galatians 3:17-18: "This is what I mean: the law, which came 430 years afterward, does not annul a covenant previously ratified by God, so as** to make the promise void. For if the inheritance comes by the law, it no longer comes by promise; but God gave it to Abraham by a promise."

God's promises are never invalidated because sinful people did not do what sinful people *cannot* do. No people, not even God's chosen people of Israel, are able to obey God's law apart from His cleansing and regeneration. What is needed is a mechanism by which Israel's sinful hearts can be made righteous and thereby prompt all the blessings still pending in the Abrahamic and Davidic covenants. This is what is promised in a fourth covenant, the *New Covenant*, as described by Jeremiah. It reads:

> 'Behold, the days are coming,' declares the LORD, 'when I will make a new covenant with the house of Israel and with the house of Judah, not like the covenant that I made with their fathers on the day when I took them by the hand to bring them out of the land of Egypt, My covenant that they broke [that is, the Mosaic Covenant] though I was their husband,' declares the LORD" (31:31-32).

In other words, in order to satisfy God's standard of holy perfection, Israel requires a "new" covenant unlike the Mosaic Covenant with its impossible demands for perfect righteousness. **Verse 33** then

33

adds: "**'For this is the covenant that I will make with the house of Israel after those days,' declares the LORD: 'I will put My law within them, and I will write it on their hearts. And I will be their God, and they shall be My people."** In a parallel passage, **Ezekiel 36:26-27** proclaims, **"And I will give you a new heart, and a new spirit I will put within you. And I will remove the heart of stone from your flesh and give you a heart of flesh. And I will put my Spirit within you, and cause you to walk in My statutes and be careful to obey My rules."**

There is a word for this: *salvation.* This is God's promise to save Israel (**Rom 11:26**). In the New Covenant, God says there will be a day when He will purify the hearts of His people sovereignly. In His Word, God promises to bless the righteous (**Ps 5:12**), but paradoxically He has declared that, **"None is righteous, no, not one"** (**Rom 3:10**). Thus, God must fix the problem of Israel's unrighteousness before He can bless her, and with the New Covenant comes God's claim that one day He will do exactly that. When the New Covenant is fulfilled, God will write His law on His chosen people's heart so that their very nature will be righteous, thereby triggering the blessings promised in the Abrahamic and Davidic Covenants.

What about Gentile believers, those outside of ethnic Israel? Do the promises of God extend to them as well? Absolutely! The Bible is unmistakable in assuring that the promises God made to Israel apply to all who repent and believe in Christ's atoning sacrifice (**Rom 10:13; Gal 3:14, 29**). Israel was never meant as the sole beneficiary of God's mercy and loving-kindness; rather, it is through Israel that salvation was intended to come to all peoples and nations (**Isa 45:22; John 4:22**). Note how the prophet Isaiah references this exact point (as God says of His Son, Jesus): **"It is too light a thing that you should be My servant to raise up the tribes of Jacob and to bring back the preserved of Israel; I will make you as a light for the nations, that My salvation may reach to the end of the earth"** (**Isa 49:6**). But note the nuance here. The glorious promise of New Covenant salvation is for all believers throughout the wider world, *but not to the exclusion of a remnant of ethnic Israel!* Rather, all believers will participate *alongside Israel* in the earthly kingdom promised to her, united under the reign of the great and coming King, Jesus Christ.

In addition to the Abrahamic, the Mosaic, the Davidic and the New Covenant, there is a fifth covenant, often neglected and forgotten but highly significant for the future of Israel, and that is the Palestinian or Deuteronomic Covenant: the pact God established with Israel on the plains of Moab (**Deut 27-30**).[2] The Deuteronomic Covenant promised Israel rights to the Promised Land. Hence, it had a related theme to the previous Covenants made to Israel: the

Abrahamic gave the title deed to the land; the Mosaic provided a constitution for the people of the land; and the Deuteronomic would delineate Israel's rights and riches of their Promised land. In each covenant the literal land of Canaan was at issue—and it was given to Israel as a gift from God (**Deut 3:18**). God had the right to give it, for He owned the land. In the Deuteronomic Covenant God promised to scatter Israel among the nations if they disobeyed, which they did. In chapter 30, He then promised to one day gather them back from the ends of the earth as one people, into the land of Promise. At that time, He will give them a new heart to obey and love God and they will dwell in the land that He promised them. This latter promise remains to be fulfilled.

The bottom line? In the future, a generation of ethnic Jews will come to faith in Jesus Christ collectively as a people. The fulfillment of the covenant promises described in this chapter awaits the salvation of the remnant of Jews God has ordained to eternal life since before time began. And when that happens, Jesus will return to deliver to them their promised kingdom. **Zechariah 12:10** poignantly describes how God will pour out upon Israel, **"a spirit of grace and pleas for mercy, so that, when they look upon Me, upon Him whom they have pierced, they shall mourn for Him, as one mourns for an only child, and weep bitterly over Him, as one weeps over a firstborn."** And what will be the result? **Zechariah 13:1: "On that day there shall be a fountain opened for the house of David and the inhabitants of Jerusalem, to cleanse them from sin and uncleanness."**

A physical kingdom is coming for ethnic Israel, in a literal territory with earthly designations, to be ruled by Jesus Christ, the eternal King. God has promised this to His chosen people, Israel—the ethnic descendants of Abraham, Isaac and Jacob—in a series of unilateral, unconditional, irrevocable covenants to which He is sworn (**Heb 6:13-20**). All people who come to saving faith in the Lord Jesus Christ on the basis of the New Covenant will share in the inheritance of the coming earthly kingdom of Christ (and in His eternal kingdom to follow), but *not* in a manner that replaces ethnic Israel. In the next chapter, we explore a particularly important prophecy regarding Israel's future fate as it relates to the end of the world.

3

DANIEL LOOKS AHEAD

As we have seen, the history of Israel and her designation by God as His chosen nation fills much of the Old Testament; it can be framed by the distinct covenants God made with her—unconditional, unilateral, irrevocable promises from God to Israel involving her establishment as a nation, with distinct land boundaries. Furthermore, Israel was promised both to receive and to impart divine blessing. Not only that, God has also promised Israel a future earthly kingdom, with her King reigning from Jerusalem. Finally, God has promised He will eventually renew the hearts of His chosen people, so that they might repent and turn to Jesus Christ, the Promised Messiah rejected by their forbearers, thereby triggering all the other promised blessings.

One passage in particular, **Daniel 9:24-27**, directly addresses Israel's relationship to the world's end. Sir

Isaac Newton once claimed that one could stake the truth of Christianity on this prophecy alone.[1] Jesus referenced this prophecy as being foundational in His most definitive explanation of the chronology of end time events (**Matt 24**). No one's theology of future events is complete without it. It reads:

> [24]**Seventy weeks** [lit. *sevens*] **are decreed about your people and your holy city, to finish the transgression, to put an end to sin, and to atone for iniquity, to bring in everlasting righteousness, to seal both vision and prophet, and to anoint a most holy place.** [25]**Know therefore and understand that from the going out of the word to restore and build Jerusalem to the coming of an Anointed One, a Prince; there shall be seven weeks** [lit. *sevens*] **Then for sixty–two weeks** [lit. *sevens*] **it shall be built again with squares and a moat, but in a troubled time.**
>
> [26]**And after the sixty-two weeks** [lit. *sevens*] **an Anointed One shall be cut off and shall have nothing. And the people of the prince who is to come shall destroy the city and the sanctuary. Its end shall come with a flood, and to the end there shall be war. Desolations are determined.**

²⁷And he shall make a strong covenant with many for one week [lit. *sevens*] and for half of the week he shall put an end to sacrifice and offering. And on the wing of abominations shall come one who makes desolate, until the decreed end is poured out on the desolator.

Hebrew scholars agree that these four verses are very challenging for the Bible exegete and interpreter, for several reasons. The main one is probably due to the fact that this prophecy conflates the two comings of Christ that we know today in hindsight have been separated by at least 2,000 years. Daniel and the Old Testament saints did not think of two comings—they only perceived one. The discontinuity—termed *prophetic foreshortening*—that results from two Messianic comings separated by a huge gap of time put a huge monkey wrench in everyone's eschatology. It is the greatest cause for the inimitable complexities and idiosyncrasies involved in trying to sort out Bible prophecy, especially chronology and timing (**1 Pet 1:11**). Nevertheless, from careful exegesis, attending to the immediate context and guided by the guardrails of the analogy of Scripture, there is much that comes across loud and clear from this passage to help inform our eschatology.

As we have seen earlier, Daniel is writing around 539 B.C. He had been in exile more than sixty years. The angel Gabriel gave him a prophecy about a time coming for Israel which will be made up of **"seventy weeks"** (**9:24**). A better, more literal translation of the Hebrew construction is "seventy sevens." The second word in the phrase is versatile and literally means "a unit of seven" or "a heptad." This Hebrew word "has no primary reference to time periods at all, whether days or years. In other words, it is simply a numerical measure."[2] This seems strange to the modern-day English reader. We tend to think in terms of tens or decades. Daniel's people thought in terms of sevens or heptads. Every seventh year was a sabbath (**Lev 25**). Every seven "sevens," or forty-nine years, brought them the mandatory Year of Jubilee (**25:8-12**). Seventy "sevens" here for Daniel referred to 490 years, the time remaining until the culmination of God's promises for Israel and for all believers.

The prophecy is a promise made **"about your people and for your holy city,"** that is, to Israel and Jerusalem (**9:24**). Next, six infinitives tell us what the Messiah will accomplish for His people. The six infinitives have an obvious syntactical structural symmetry in several respects in the Hebrew text. The infinitives are written in two sets of three; the first three are stated negatively and the second three are stated positively. The first three are two-word phrases in Hebrew; the second three are three-word phrases in

Hebrew. The first set of three is related to *sin* and is fulfilled with Christ's first coming when He came as the Suffering Servant and Sin-Bearer as He died on the cross. The last set of three is related to *righteousness* and is fulfilled in full when Christ returns at the end of the age as the Conquering King and Righteous Judge. The first three speak of Christ's now past spiritual atoning work, which is the basis of all His promises that will be fulfilled by Israel. The last three infinitives address His still earthly Kingdom promises that Israel will inherit upon its national repentance (**Deut 30:1-6; Rom 11:26**). Let's look at this in closer detail.

Christ's first coming culminated with His conquest of "the transgression" putting an end to sin's power and its consequence—death. Through His crucifixion and resurrection, the capstone of His first appearance, Christ atoned for sin and so triumphed over its damning effect. When He appears again to rule over His kingdom on earth, Jesus will **"anoint the most holy place"** with His presence in Jerusalem, which will be the epicenter of all worship (**Dan 9:24**). From that time on, righteousness will be the rule, in both the Millennium Kingdom and in the Eternal Kingdom to follow. No longer will there be any need for prophecy or visions, because God will commune directly with His people forevermore.

As for the timing of all this, Daniel writes that from the time of the decree to go and rebuild Jerusalem to the time when the first **"Prince"** will come (a name for Jesus), there will be a total of seven weeks of sevens (49 years), followed by sixty-two weeks of sevens (434 years), for a total of sixty-nine weeks of sevens (483 years). After this, Daniel prophesies that the first Prince will be **"cut off and shall have nothing,"** and a second **"prince"** shall appear (a reference to the antichrist). It is important to note that the **"Prince"** in **9:25** is a different person than the **"prince"** in **9:26**. This second prince, or Antichrist, will persecute the nation of Israel and all who follow the one true God, until the time of his decreed end (**Rev 13:1-10**).

To understand how this passage links Israel and the world's future, recall that the Babylonian empire conquered Jerusalem in 605 B.C. Beginning that year and continuing in two subsequent deportations, the people of Judah were taken into captivity. As already presented, this captivity had been foretold by the prophet Jeremiah (**25:11; 29:10**). It was to last seventy years, after which the Jews would be allowed to return home. Aware of this prophecy, Daniel perceived the time for Israel's release was drawing near, if the starting date was the first deportation in 605 B.C. As the seventy years were ending, the Medes and Persians conquered Babylon and became overseers of the Jewish captives. Under the Medo-Persian reign of Cyrus, the people of Israel were finally allowed to return to their native land, precisely as God's Word to

Jeremiah had predicted (**Ezra 1:1-3; 2 Chron 36:22-23**).

This return was permitted over a series of four decrees. The first three of these decrees (discussed in **Ezra 1, 6,** and **7**) allowed Israel to return and rebuild her fallen temple, but—interestingly—her people were *not* permitted to rebuild the city of Jerusalem itself. That had to wait until the fourth decree, under the Emperor Artaxerxes—the same Artaxerxes who ruled at the time of Esther. His decree permitting God's people to begin rebuilding Jerusalem—and in particular, to restore its perimeter walls—came around March (Nisan) 444/445 B.C. (**Neh 2:1-6**).

Now notice the following about Daniel's prophecy. He writes that there will be sixty-nine weeks of years, or 483 years, before an **"Anointed One"** (**9:25**), a reference to the Messiah, who comes and [then] He is **"cut off,"** meaning "killed." Daniel breaks this period into a time of seven weeks, followed by sixty-two weeks, for a total of sixty-nine weeks of years (or 483 years). The first seven-week period, or 49 years, is the period of time for the rebuilding of the city of Jerusalem (**v 25a**).

By this date, four special features regarding the nation of Israel deserve mention:

First, the people of Israel are back in their land of Palestine. A remnant has returned. The nation is restored.

Second, the temple is rebuilt. It would later be destroyed and again rebuilt, but for now the temple is reconstructed and functioning, with sacrifices to God resuming on its altar.

Third, the city of Jerusalem is reconstructed. It had been decimated by Nebuchadnezzar in 605 B.C., but now it is reestablished and inhabited. So the people of Israel had their nation, their temple, and their city all restored to them.

Lastly, the people of Israel had their canon. With the writings of the prophet Ezra concluded, the Old Testament was complete. God's people had His Word, the Old Testament Scripture, in its finished form. With that, God's special revelation to His people ceases, at least for a time.

That ends the first of seven "weeks" of years (i.e. 49 years from 445 B.C. to 396 B.C.). What follows is a time of silence, when the voice of God, as spoken through the prophets to His people, is abruptly halted. This time of "silence" represents the sixty-two weeks of years mentioned by Daniel. Historically, during this period, the Greeks overtake the Medes and Persians as the third great world empire (also prophesied by Daniel; cf. chaps. **2** and **7**). One of the Greek emperors to reign during this interlude is Antiochus IV "Epiphanes," whose vile torment of the people of Israel and desecration of her temple is part of the **"troubled time"** prophesied by Daniel as destined to come upon Israel (cf. **9:25**).[3]

Following the seven plus sixty-two weeks, or sixty-nine weeks, Daniel then prophesies that an **"Anointed One"** will come like a **"Prince."** This is nothing less than a prediction of Christ's first coming (the Hebrew word "Messiah" means "anointed one"). In other words, God asserts through Daniel that the Messiah will arrive after 69 weeks of years, or 483 years, from the time of the decree to rebuild Jerusalem. Astoundingly, during Passover week around AD 33 Jesus mounted a colt and rode it from nearby Bethany right into Jerusalem as the acclaimed Prince, the Messiah, in precise fulfillment of this and other Old Testament prophecies (cf. **Zech 9:9**)—exactly 483 years from the date of Artaxerxes' decree![4] This remarkable fulfillment of prophecy is an extraordinary verification that God is providentially overseeing His entire world with meticulous precision and perfect mastery.

Finally, Daniel prophesies that shortly thereafter, the Messiah will be suddenly **"cut off"** (**Dan 9:26**) from His people (an allusion to Christ's death), followed by the arrival of a **"prince who is to come"** (**Dan 9:26**). This second prince is the *Antichrist*. His ascent and his destruction all transpire during the **"one week"** of prophecy yet unfulfilled, Israel's "seventieth week," a week of seven years to bring about the end of this world as we know it.[5]

In summary, it is helpful to clarify Daniel's use and meaning of the various references to "sevens" in this complex prophetic passage just surveyed:

a) **"seventy years"** (**9:2**) refers to the number of years Jeremiah predicted Israel would be exiled in Babylon as a consequence for violating 70 sabbath year observances required by the Law (cf. **Lev 25:2-5; 2 Chron 36:21**);

b) **"seventy weeks"** (**9:24**) means "seventy sevens" and equals 490 years. The 490 years refers to the total time it will take before the Messiah comes to deal a final blow to sin and fulfill all promises made to Israel. This 490-year period corresponds exactly to the penalty required in the Law (**cf. Lev 25:2-5; 26:34-43**) for violating the sabbath year 70 different times during the 800 years in which Israel was in the land beginning with Joshua until the Babylonian captivity. Daniel goes on to divide these **"seventy weeks"** into three sections, with a prophetic event being fulfilled with each section along the way until the ultimate climax that transpires at the close of the 490 years. Incremental, telescopic or staged fulfillments are typical of biblical prophecy;

c) **"seven weeks"** (**9:25**) means seven sevens, or 49 years. This period most likely pertains to the time it actually took from the issuing of the decree until the restoration of Jerusalem which began with the decree issued in the days of Nehemiah;[6]

d) **"sixty-two weeks"** (**9:25, 26**) means sixty-two sevens or 434 years and comprises the time from the rebuilding of Jerusalem to the first coming of the Messiah (**v. 25 b**);

e) **"seven weeks and sixty-two weeks"** (**9:25**) means sixty-nine sevens, or 483 years. This is the time-period from the decree of Cyrus to the death of Christ. There is purposely a gap between the 69th week and the 70th week in light of Christ's two comings.

f) **"one week"** (**9:27**) means one seven or seven years, and refers to the seven-year Tribulation at the end of the world before Christ's Second coming. Daniel says this week is typified by the presence of the Antichrist whom he calls **"the prince"** (**9:26**), **"a little horn"** (**7:8**), **"a man"** (**7:8**), with a **"mouth which spoke pompous words"** (**7:20**), who **"will make war against the saints"** (**7:21**), who will be a **"king"** (**7:24**), who will **"speak blasphemies"** (**11:36**). He will make a covenant with Israel at the beginning of the 70th week (**9:27a**).

g) **"the middle of the week"** (**9:27**) means the middle of the seven, or half of seven years. Three-and-a-half years into the covenant he made with Israel, the Antichrist will break that covenant and turn against the Jews and then dominate for another three-and-a-half years. Jesus called this time of domination the **"Great Tribulation"** (**Matt 24:21**). Revelation said it would last 42 months (**13:5**), or **"a time and times and half a time,"** (**12:14**) or 1,260 days (**12:6**)—all the same as 3 ½ years.

We will see how the remainder of Daniel's amazing prophecy comes to fruition in chapter 7.

4

SIGNS OF THE LAST DAY

Perhaps the most common question arising from those who desire to know what the Bible says about the future is, "Do you think the end is near?" After all, it has been over 2500 years since God unveiled His New Covenant for salvation to His chosen people of Israel (and by extension, to all those who are children of Abraham by faith; cf. **Gal 3:29**). Moreover, it has been nearly 2000 years since the Son of God, Jesus Christ, triumphed over sin and death via His crucifixion, resurrection, and ascension, *propitiating* God's wrath, *expiating* the penitent believer's sin, and—critically for our topic—*introducing* the indwelling presence of the Holy Spirit. The Bible announces this last development as the triggering event for the **"last days"** (**Amos 2:17; Joel 2:28; Acts 2:16-21**).

So the Bible's answer to this predominating question is an unequivocal, "Yes." Peter, Paul, James, Jude and the writer of Hebrews all stipulate under inspiration of God that **"the end of the ages has come"** (**1 Cor 10:11**) and that **"the end of all things is at hand"** (**1 Pet 4:7**; see also **Heb 1:2**; **James 5:3**; **Jude 1:18**). No less an expert on eschatology than Jesus Christ, in revealing the closing events of the world to the Apostle John around A.D. 95 or 96, said of their imminent launch, **"the time is near"** (**Rev 1:3**). Undoubtedly for this reason, the Apostle John describes the time of his writing as **"the last hour"** (**1 John 2:18**). But how *far* into that hour are we? Here we can turn to God's specific descriptions of earthly developments that will herald the end. What does the Bible say life will be like as creation comes to a close?

Unfortunately, God's Word is clear that as the end draws nigh, things in this world will be going from bad to worse (**2 Tim 3:13**). James says the time will be marked by the idolatry of wealth (**5:3**). Jude foresees **"scoffers, following their own ungodly passions"** (**Jude 1:18**). Peter says sinful desires will lead these scoffers to a host of impudent disavowals, including denial of the imminent return of Christ, denial of God's literal rendering of creation, denial of the Noahic flood, and denial of the future destruction of the universe (**2 Pet 3:3-7**). Paul agrees as he writes:

> **But understand this, that in the last days there will come times of difficulty. For people will be lovers of self, lovers of money, proud, arrogant, abusive,**

disobedient to their parents, ungrateful, unholy, heartless, unappeasable, slanderous, without self-control, brutal, not loving good, treacherous, reckless, swollen with conceit, lovers of pleasure rather than lovers of God, having the appearance of godliness, but denying its power (2 Tim 3:1-5).

Paul goes on to say people, **"will be burdened with sins and led astray by various passions, always learning and never able to arrive at a knowledge of the truth"** (vv. 6b-7). These same individuals will, **"oppose the truth, men corrupted in mind and disqualified regarding the faith"** (v. 8). In another passage, Paul describes the course of the human condition on earth as marked by foolish and futile thinking and by hearts that have become darkened, leading to a progressive and shameless decline into all forms of sexual immorality (**Rom 1:21-27**). And what is the endpoint? Paul continues:

And since they did not see fit to acknowledge God, God gave them up to a debased mind to do what ought not to be done. They were filled with all manner of unrighteousness, evil, covetousness, malice. They are full of envy, murder, strife, deceit, maliciousness. They are gossips,

slanderers, haters of God, insolent, haughty, boastful, inventors of evil, disobedient to parents, foolish, faithless, heartless, ruthless. Though they know God's righteous decree that those who practice such things deserve to die, they not only do them but give approval to those who practice them (Rom 1:28-32).

Notice in particular that this deterioration of society is not only among those outside the Church. The Bible is clear that there will be those who profess faith—those **"having the appearance of godliness" (2 Tim 3:5)**—who will contribute toward this decline into greater and greater depravity. The pernicious deviation from sound doctrine by some within the professing church is encompassed in the term *apostasy*. Its sinister and malignant effect is the reason why the Bible continually warns believers to be on guard against those within the Church who would alter the Word of God, and in particular the gospel (**Acts 20:28-31; Gal 1:6-10; Eph. 5:11; 1 Tim 6:20; 2 Tim 4:1-4; Titus 1:9; 2 Pet 2:1-22; 2 John 7-11; Jude 3-23**). In fact, in **1 Timothy 4:1**, Paul writes, **"Now the Spirit expressly says that in later times some will depart from the faith by devoting themselves to deceitful spirits and teachings of demons...."** And what are the teachings of demons? Any ideas raised against the true person and purpose of God, as written in His Word (**2 Cor 10:5; James 3:14-15**).

The common characteristic of those contributing to this degenerative spiral—both among those who profess to believe and those who flat-out reject—will be their *denial of truth*. Recall above how Paul describes them as, **"always learning and never able to arrive at a knowledge of the truth"** (**2 Tim 3:7**). They are those who will, being corrupted in mind, **"oppose the truth"** (**v. 8**). In his letter to the Romans, Paul writes, **"For the wrath of God is revealed from heaven against all ungodliness and unrighteousness of men, who by their unrighteousness *suppress the truth*"** (**Rom 1:18**; emphasis added). Opposition to truth reaches its nadir when what is true is actually labeled as false, and what is false is labeled as true. Addressing this, the prophet Isaiah warns, **"Woe to those who call evil good and good evil, who put darkness for light and light for darkness, who put bitter for sweet and sweet for bitter!"** (**Isa 5:20**).

That the enemies of God would be characterized by their disdain for and rejection of truth follows the logical progression of Scripture. For if Jesus says that those who follow Him are sanctified by the truth of God's Word (**John 8:31-32; 17:17**), then it stands to reason that those who reject Him would be identified as deniers of that same truth. In any event, the consequence of rebelling against God's truth is at once both startling and sobering. In **2 Thessalonians 2:10-**

12, Paul describes those who are ultimately perishing as those who **"refused to love the truth and so be saved."** He then continues: **"Therefore, God sends them a strong delusion, so that they may believe what is false, in order that all may be condemned who did not believe the truth but had pleasure in unrighteousness."** Here we learn there comes a time when *God actually reinforces the delusion of those who rebel against Him,* because of their persistent effrontery in snubbing His truth. It is a fearful thing to reject the great mercy of God by rejecting His truth about the path to salvation, for beyond that there is no other mercy available, but only judgment (cf. **John 3:18; 36; Heb 10:31; Rev 21:6-8**).

So are we near the end? Consider the following: Is wealth idolized? Are scoffers mocking the biblical account of the return of Christ, a six-day literal creation scheme, a worldwide Noahic flood and the coming destruction of the universe? Are sexual immoralities and other forms of ungodliness rampant? Is right being characterized as wrong, and wrong as right? Is God's truth being desecrated by professing but false believers, committed hedonists, and all those in between? These are the signs that will herald the beginning of the end.

5

RAPTURE

The first event that will interrupt this societal decline is known as the *Rapture*. The Rapture is the first of six events in the order of last things. It is the gathering of all Church Age believers—both the living and the dead—into the presence of the Lord. The term "Rapture" derives from the Greek verb *harpazo* which means "to snatch up." **First Thessalonians 4:16-17** says all who are **"in Christ"** will be **"caught up"** together to meet the Lord in the air. **First Thessalonians 4:13-18** describes the event:

> [13]**But we do not want you to be uninformed, brothers, about those who are asleep, that you may not grieve as others do who have no hope. [14]For since we believe that Jesus died and rose again, even so, through Jesus, God will bring with him those who have fallen**

asleep. [15]For this we declare to you by a word from the Lord, that we who are alive, who are left until the coming of the Lord, will not precede those who have fallen asleep. [16]For the Lord Himself will descend from heaven with a cry of command, with the voice of an archangel, and with the sound of the trumpet of God. And the dead in Christ will rise first. [17]Then we who are alive, who are left, will be caught up together with them in the clouds to meet the Lord in the air, and so we will always be with the Lord. [18]Therefore encourage one another with these words.

With respect to the Rapture, *six aspects* should be understood in anticipation of this wonderful event.

First, the Rapture is *imminent,* meaning that it comes next. You might wonder what the Bible says must occur before the Rapture, and the answer is nothing. It comes next, and it could come at any time. The Rapture is a *sign-less event,* meaning that there are no signs or developments that must precede its occurrence.

Second, the Rapture is *inevitable.* Despite the multiple biblical passages predicting this event, some professing believers still deny the coming sudden removal of God's true Church from the Earth. But notice how Paul links knowledge of the Rapture with knowledge of Christ's death and resurrection (**v. 14**). Paul is saying if you believe Christ died and rose again, then by the same token you should believe in the coming Rapture of the saints.

Third, the Rapture occurs *in the air*. The text says those both dead and alive will be **"caught up together…in the clouds to meet the Lord in the air"** (**v. 17**). This fulfills the prophecy spoken by the angels to the Apostles as they gazed into heaven at the Ascension of Christ:

> **…as they were looking on, He was lifted up, and a cloud took Him out of their sight. And while they were gazing into heaven as he went, behold, two men stood by them in white robes, and said, "Men of Galilee, why do you stand looking into heaven? This Jesus, who was taken up from you into heaven, will come in the same way as you saw Him go into heaven" (Acts 1:9-11).**

A cloud took the Lord Jesus into heaven at His ascension. And in that same manner, Jesus will come from heaven for His believers, as they rise to join Him in the air.

Fourth, this Rapture of the Church to meet Christ in the air is *different from the Second Coming of Christ*. In the Rapture, Christ's followers rise to meet Him in the air as He descends in the clouds. Later, at His Second Coming, Christ will also descend in the clouds, but then He will not remain in the air but will descend all the way down to Earth. **Zechariah 14:4** declares on that day, Jesus' feet shall stand upon the Mount of Olives, which will then split to form a great valley. But, as we shall see, this is still to come.

Fifth, the Rapture is *for believers*, involving a *Reckoning*, a *Reward*, and a *Resurrection*:

Reckoning—the Rapture may be when Church age believers appear before the Lord, at what is called the *Bema* judgment or Judgment Seat of Christ, to give an account of all they have ever done (**Rom 14:10, 12; 2 Cor 5:10**).[1] Paul writes in **Romans 14:10** that **"we will all stand before the judgment seat of God"** and that **"each of us will give an account of himself to God"** (**v. 12**). Here, one must remember the Rapture is about uniting the Church with Christ. None of the Rapture passages in Scripture (**John 14:3; 1 Cor 15:50-58; Col 3:4; 1 Thess 4:13-18; Rev 3:10**) mention any hint of punishment. While believers will regret the myriad ways they have grieved God, the *bema* judgment is not a time when believers will be punished for their sins, for there is no threat of condemnation in light of Christ's atoning work on their behalf (**Rom 8:1**). For those who are redeemed, all the sins committed during one's life—both prior to and following salvation—were forgiven at the cross. Because of this, the joy of believers at finally experiencing the physical presence of the Lord will overwhelm any real but fleeting shame that comes as they review their earthly transgressions. **First John 2:28** says, **"And now, little children, abide in Him, so that when He appears we may have confidence and not shrink from Him in shame at His coming."** This is meant as an encouragement for believers to remain steadfast, living in a holy and upright manner, so that they might not be ashamed when Christ appears.

Rewards—after the Rapture is when believers receive their *rewards*. **First Corinthians 3:13-14 says, "each one's work will become manifest, for the Day will disclose it, because it will be revealed by fire, and the fire will test what sort of work each one has done. If the work that anyone has built on the foundation survives, he will receive a reward."** When Jesus references reward or recompense, He is not talking about the believer's salvation. Believers do not receive salvation for what *they* have done; they receive salvation for what *Christ* has done. So these are distinct rewards beyond salvation, which Christ has promised for faithful work done while His physical presence has been away (cf. **Matt 5:12; 25:14-30; Luke 14:14; 19:11-27; Col 3:24; 2 John 1:8**).

Resurrection—the Rapture is when believers in Christ, both dead and alive, receive their *glorified bodies*. Paul describes this vividly in one of the most glorious passages in the entire Bible:

> **⁵¹Behold! I tell you a mystery. We shall not all sleep, but we shall all be changed, ⁵²in a moment, in the twinkling of an eye, at the last trumpet. For the trumpet will sound, and the dead will be raised imperishable, and we shall be changed (1 Cor 15:51-52).**

It is very likely that Paul is describing the Rapture event in this passage. He calls it a "mystery" (**v. 51**) meaning here he is giving new information that was not revealed in the Old Testament. The resurrection was revealed in the Old Testament (**Ps 16; Isa 26:19-20; Dan 12:2; Heb 11:19**), so that is not the new information. The mystery is that some people will get a perfect, immortal, supernatural, glorified body without first having to die and then be resurrected! That concept was never taught in the Old Testament.

What is meant in saying the believer will receive a "resurrection body?" The Bible declares that when one dies his or her spirit immediately leaves its physical body and goes to its spiritual assignment, either to heaven to be with the Lord (cf. **Luke 23:43; 2 Cor 5:8; Phil 1:23**), or to hell to be reserved until the Day of Judgment (cf. **Luke 16:22-23**). In other words, there is no such thing as Purgatory, or "soul sleep."

Next, the Bible teaches that *everyone*—both the redeemed and the unredeemed—will eventually undergo a resurrection, when one's spirit will be reunited with a body (cf. **John 5:28-29**; **Rev 20:5-6**). The frail living bodies of Church saints will be "translated" or "transformed" (**Phil 3:21**) on the spot at the Rapture. Their mortal bodies will instantly become glorified supernatural bodies while they are still alive. These bodies will never taste death or decay throughout eternity, nor will they ever be capable of sinning.

As for how these bodies are allocated, the Bible lists different *stages* or times of resurrection for different groups. And the stage or time of resurrection—when a person receives his or her eternal body—will depend on whether that person is *redeemed* or not. Furthermore, among the *redeemed*, the time of resurrection will depend upon the era or period during which the believer lived. Paul said there was an "order" to resurrection (**1 Cor 15:23**), meaning not every person gets their resurrection body at the same time; there is a chronological sequence. Thus, the order of resurrection is as follows: 1) Christ is the firstfruits of resurrection (**1 Cor 15:23**); 2) Old Testament saints buried around Jerusalem were raised immediately after Jesus died on Friday (**Matt 27:52-53**); 3) Christians at the time of the Rapture (**1 Thess 4:16**); 4) the two witnesses murdered during the Tribulation (**Rev 11:11-12**); 5) the rest of the Old Testament saints and Tribulation martyrs (**Isa 26:19; Dan 12:2; Rev 6:9-11; 20:4**); 6) Millennial saints (**John 5:28-29; Rev 20:6**); the unredeemed of all the ages at the Great White Throne (**Rev 20:5, 11-15**). Our resurrection bodies will be patterned after Jesus' resurrection body (**Phil 3:21**). It's incredible to imagine that Jesus, the eternal One, who had no physical body prior to being born through Mary, will retain His physical resurrection body for all eternity and at the same time He has all the attributes of deity, including omnipresence.

Finally, there is a *sixth* and crucial point about the Rapture: it *removes the Spirit's restraining influence from the world*. Believe it or not this world is not as bad as it can be—actually, not even close. But someday the world will be at its worst—rampant wickedness like never seen before. Jesus said so (**Matt 24:21**). The world isn't as bad as it might be now because of the ongoing ministry of the Holy Spirit who is currently restraining evil in the world through conscience, world governments, the Church, prayer, and the influence of His indwelling presence in individual believers, who are a preserving salt and light in a corrupt world (**Phil 2:15**). In the future the Holy Spirit will remove all His restraining forces and let evil run amuck. This removal will be triggered at the Rapture. **Second Thessalonians 2:7** says, **"For the mystery of lawlessness is already at work. Only He who now restrains it will do so until He is out of the way."** To understand how the Rapture triggers an upsurge in evil upon the earth, recall the present dwelling place of the Holy Spirit—*within the hearts of believers* (cf. **John**

14:17; Rom 8:9-11; Eph 1:13). With the removal of all true believers from the earth at the Rapture, the Spirit's presence—and thus His restraining influence—is also removed. In other words, as the Spirit departs with the raptured believers in whom He dwells, so His restraint of evil also departs—that is the gist of **2 Thessalonians 2:7**. And this crescendo of evil coinciding with the Spirit's departure which sets in motion the next event in the order of last things: the Tribulation.

6

TRIBULATION

The *Tribulation* is the seven-year period that follows the Rapture of the Church. It is a time of horrific judgment brought by God upon the earth. Jesus says of that time, **"In those days there will be such tribulation as has not been from the beginning of the creation that God created until now, and never will be"** (**Mark 13:19**). Jesus called it a **"great tribulation"** (**Matt 24:21**) as does the book of Revelation (**7:14**).

How do we know the Tribulation will last for seven years? Recall the prophecy of **Daniel 9:24-27**, from Chapter 3. We learned that from the time of the decree of Artaxerxes permitting the people of Israel to rebuild Jerusalem until the coming of the anointed One as He rode into Jerusalem would be a duration of 69 weeks of years, or 483 years. But the beginning of that prophecy in **Daniel 9:24** promises 70 "sevens" (or "weeks of years"), or 490 years, until the end of all things would come. This means one "week" of years, or seven years, is missing—a week of years yet to come. This is the **"one week"** referred to in **Daniel 9:27**, the seven-year period known as the Tribulation.

Much is written in both the Old and New Testaments concerning this seven-year Tribulation. To distill this information as concisely as possible, consider the following *eight fundamentals* for understanding the *Tribulation*:

1) its *Purpose*;
2) its *Prelude*;
3) its *Pretender*;
4) its *Progression*;
5) its *Pivot Point*;
6) its *Protection*;
7) its *Perils*; and
8) its *Promise*.

First, we consider the *Purpose* of the Tribulation. What is God's intent in ordaining this seven-year period at the end of the age? The Bible actually relates a *three-fold* purpose for the coming Tribulation. One main purpose of the Tribulation is that it is intended as a *time of chastening for the people of Israel*, described by the prophet Jeremiah as the **"time of Jacob's trouble"** (**Jer 30:7; KJV**). During this time God will chasten or discipline Israel like a loving Father toward His children; it will not be a time of condemnation toward Israel—there's a difference. And why will they be chastened? They will be chastened to woo them to repentance for their ages-long disobedience against God, culminating in their rejection of Jesus as the Messiah (**Lev 26:40-45**). **Ezekiel 20:33-38** depicts God's coming judgment against Israel in the Tribulation:

> **'As I live,' declares the Lord GOD, 'surely with a mighty hand and an outstretched arm and with wrath poured out, I shall be King over you. I will bring you out from the peoples and gather you out of the countries where you are scattered, with a mighty hand and an outstretched arm and with wrath poured out. And I will bring you into the wilderness of the peoples, and there I will enter into judgment with you face to face.**

> **'As I entered into judgment with your fathers in the wilderness of the land of Egypt, so I will enter into judgment with you,' declares the Lord GOD. 'I will make you pass under the rod, and I will bring you into the bond of the covenant. I will purge out the rebels from among you and those who transgress against Me. I will bring them out of the land where they sojourn, but**

> **they shall not enter the land of Israel. Then you will know that I am the LORD.'**

The second main purpose of the Tribulation is to judge *the nations of the world*, as punishment for their rebellion against God (cf. **Rev 3:10**). **Isaiah 13:11** is one of many passages declaring God's eschatological judgment against the nations at the end of world history: **"I** [God] **will punish the world for its evil, and the wicked for their iniquity; I will put an end to the pomp of the arrogant, and lay low the pompous pride of the ruthless."** This will come to pass during the Tribulation.

But even as He metes out His punishment upon a disbelieving Israel and a sinful world, God displays His great mercy to the very end. So, lastly, there is a third purpose of the Tribulation—it is God's one last time for calling all sinners to repentance—*Jews and Gentiles alike.* **Revelation 7** says that during the time of the Tribulation 144,000 Jews—12,000 from every tribe— will be witnesses of the gospel to the world. In response to this testimony, **verse 9** declares, **"a great multitude that no one could number, from every nation, from all tribes and peoples and languages"** will come to faith, many of whom will subsequently be martyred for the very same faith.

As to the *Prelude* to the Tribulation, what initiates this seven-year period? The answer lies in **Revelation**

5:1-14. In this passage, God is seated upon His throne, holding in His hand a *scroll*, the will of God regarding the consummation of His Kingdom on earth. As already covered in the Introduction, God rules over His entire creation eternally. However, within God's all-encompassing rule, He has permitted, for a time, a tiny speck of rebellion on Earth. Heading this rebellion is the devil, who has been delegated limited authority until the time when God's purposes for such a rebellion are concluded (cf. **1 John 5:19**).

Now is that time. In this scene, Jesus, the Lion of the Tribe of Judah, the Root of David, approaches the throne of His Father and takes the scroll, the content of which amounts to what transpires from Revelation chapter 6 on as each of the seven seals on the scroll are peeled away. This momentous action represents Jesus assuming full control of Earth, once and for all. The devil was permitted to meddle for a time in order to accomplish the sovereign purposes of God, but no longer. The Tribulation is the period when Christ begins fulfilling His role as promised in the Davidic Covenant wherein the Messiah establishes His Kingdom and righteousness on the earth as it is in heaven.

We are about to see what Christ's unrolling of the scroll means for the world, but before we get there, we have to meet the *Pretender* of the Tribulation, who is none other than the *Antichrist*. In **2 Thessalonians**

2:3-8, Paul describes this man, along with the times and events that lead to his ascendency:

> **Let no one deceive you in any way. For that day will not come, unless the rebellion comes first, and the man of lawlessness is revealed, the son of destruction, who opposes and exalts himself against every so-called god or object of worship, so that he takes his seat in the temple of God, proclaiming himself to be God. Do you not remember that when I was still with you I told you these things? And you know what is restraining him now so that he may be revealed in his time. For the mystery of lawlessness is already at work. Only He who now restrains it** [remember, that is the Holy Spirit] **will do so until He is out of the way. And then the lawless one will be revealed.**

So the lawless one, the Antichrist, comes after the withdrawal of the Spirit's restraining influence in the world. Paul goes on to write, **"The coming of the lawless one is by the activity of Satan with all power and false signs and wonders, and with all wicked deception for those who are perishing, because they refused to love the truth and so be saved"** (**vv. 9-10**). Two developments are thus occurring simultaneously. In heaven, Christ obtains the scroll, the final judgments coming to the earth, which He is about to unroll, bringing universal destruction. And at the same time, on Earth, things are going from bad to worse, until the time comes when the Antichrist rises to a position of authority over all the world (**Dan 11:36-45**).

We now come to the *Progression* of the Tribulation, which Jesus relates in His Olivet Discourse (cf. **Matt 24:9-35; Luke 21:8-32; Mark 13:5-31**) and is described in even greater detail in **Revelation 6-19**. Here is the sequence of the Tribulation: the scroll, which Jesus holds, is itself held together by seven *seals*. Each of these seals represents a distinct development upon the earth during the Tribulation. As each seal is opened in heaven, that development occurs on the earth. When the seventh seal is opened, it elicits seven "trumpet" judgments, and the seventh trumpet judgment contains seven "bowls of wrath" judgments poured out upon the earth. So the seals are broken in regular sequence, but when you get to the seventh seal, which are the seven trumpet judgments, the pace of God's judgment upon the earth quickens. And by the time you get to the seventh trumpet judgment, containing the seven bowls of wrath, the events are all coming in rapid-fire succession.

The Seal Judgments

As the Tribulation commences, we see the first four seals revealing four successive horses, each with its own rider, the "four horsemen of the Apocalypse." With the opening of the *first seal* comes a rider on a white horse, holding a bow but no arrows. This horse and rider represent the world's general fascination with peace, regardless of its price or permanence. This false peace will be coordinated by a succession of false messiahs (cf. **Matt 24:3-5**), culminating with the Antichrist.[1] He makes a false peace with Israel at the outset of the Tribulation, and pretends to offer her security. **Daniel 9:27** says this covenant of protection with Israel will last for one week, understood as one seven-year period.

The worldwide illusion of peace is broken, however, with the opening of the *second seal,* which is represented by a rider on a red horse, bringing war upon the earth. The *third seal* is then opened, and a rider on a black horse is seen, bringing famine to the world. This is followed by the opening of the *fourth seal,* revealing a rider on a pale horse, bringing death to one-fourth of the world from a combination of war, famine, pestilence and "wild beasts" (cf. **Rev 6:8**).

As Christ opens the *fifth seal,* we see the martyred saints of the Tribulation crying out to God to avenge their deaths. Who are these? Recall that even though the Tribulation is a time of God's judgment upon the earth, the gospel message will still be proclaimed, and many will believe (cf. **Rev 7:9-17**). As noted previously, this evangelism will be spearheaded by 144,000 Jews, 12,000 from each tribe. They will be converted early in the Tribulation and then go about as gospel witnesses throughout the earth.[2] These saints of the fifth seal are the Tribulation converts who are martyred as a result of their newly found faith. They are depicted in **Revelation 6:9-10** as crying out to God to avenge their deaths. In response, each is given a white robe, and told to be patient a while longer, until the total number of God's chosen Tribulation martyrs are gathered in.

Now, at this period between the fifth and sixth seals, we reach the *Pivot Point* of the Tribulation. Up to now, the Antichrist has secured a false peace for the people of Israel. But at this moment, three-and-a-half years into the Tribulation, he suddenly reneges on that pledge of protection and initiates a persecution against Israel, and against all believers (**Rev 13:7**). This *Pivot Point* therefore represents the transition from the Tribulation into the Great Tribulation. Just when conditions upon the earth look altogether bleak, they become frightfully worse. How will one know when this Pivot Point comes? Jesus cautions it will come **"when you see the abomination of desolation standing where he ought not to be" (Mark 13:14).** What does He mean?

To understand Christ's warning, it is assumed that during the first half of the Tribulation, under the rubric of a "false peace" secured between the Jews and the Antichrist (**Dan 9:27**), the temple of Jerusalem will be rebuilt. There, upon this sacred place of old from which they have been excluded for many centuries, the Jews will be permitted to offer sacrifices once again. But at this Pivot Point, the sacrifices will be halted, and the Antichrist will establish *himself* as the god to be worshipped by all (this is the "abomination of desolation," spoken of by Christ in His Olivet Discourse; cf. **Matt 24:15; Mark 13:14; Dan 12:11**). **Daniel 9:27** relates that halfway through the "week" (or seven-year period of the Tribulation), **"he** [the Antichrist] **shall put an end to sacrifice and offering. And on the wing of abominations shall come one who makes desolate, until the decreed end is poured out on the desolator."** From that point on until the time of his defeat, the Antichrist will tolerate no other worship but to himself.

So the desolator is the Antichrist, and when he desecrates the temple with his abominable decree that he alone be worshipped as god, that will signal the halfway point, or Pivot Point, of the Tribulation. At that point, three-and-a-half years are concluded; there now remain three-and-a-half years, or 42 months (**Rev 13:5**), or 1260 days (**Rev 11:3; 12:6**) until the end is accomplished. At this mid-point of the Tribulation, the Antichrist will direct all his fury against the Jews (**Matt 24:15-28; Rev 11:7; 12:17**), as well as against Gentile believers (**Rev 13:7**). They will be massacred in tremendous numbers, and as they are martyred, they will join the Tribulation saints of the fifth seal judgment (**Rev 6:9-11**). But be assured of this: God will not allow all Israel to perish (**Rev 12:6**). As we have seen, they remain His chosen people to the end, for **"the gifts and the calling of God are irrevocable"** (**Rom 11:29**). God has promised an earthly Kingdom to Israel, and in order to inherit an earthly Kingdom, a subset of Jews must therefore remain alive.

And this brings us to the *Protection* of the Tribulation. God has promised that a remnant of Israel, as well as Gentile believers who are "children of Abraham by faith" (**Rom 3:29-30; Gal 3:9, 29**), will survive the furies of the Tribulation and the wrath of the Antichrist in order to enter into the earthly Kingdom promised of old (**2 Sam 7:12; Rom 11:25-32**). How many will be delivered in this manner? **Zechariah 13:8** reveals: **"In the whole land, declares the LORD, two thirds shall be cut off and perish, and one third shall be left alive."**

So God protects this remnant of believers. Next question: how does He do it? First, He gives them *instruction* as to how to respond when the Great Tribulation comes. Jesus warns those living during this time:

> **But when you see the abomination of desolation standing where he ought not**

to be (let the reader understand), then let those who are in Judea flee to the mountains. Let the one who is on the housetop not go down, nor enter his house, to take anything out, and let the one who is in the field not turn back to take his cloak. And alas for women who are pregnant and for those who are nursing infants in those days! Pray that it may not happen in winter. For in those days there will be such tribulation as has not been from the beginning of the creation that God created until now, and never will be. And if the Lord had not cut short the days, no human being would be saved. But for the sake of the elect, whom He chose, He shortened the days. And then if anyone says to you, "Look, here is the Christ!" or "Look, there He is!" do not believe it. For false christs and false prophets will arise and perform signs and wonders, to lead astray, if possible, the elect. But be on guard; I have told you all things beforehand (Mark 13:14-23).

God gives His chosen of the Tribulation this warning: they are to flee from Jerusalem when they witness the "abomination of desolation," the worship of the Antichrist in the temple.

Second, the Bible states that God will *aid their flight to safety supernaturally*. **Revelation 12:14** reveals that Israel will be given two **"wings of the great eagle"** to aid her escape. This language describes how God will providentially protect His chosen remnant in its flight from danger. Lastly, that same chapter (**Rev 12**) tells us that the forces of the Antichrist, which will come like a great flood in pursuit of Israel and other believers, will be supernaturally *swallowed up by the earth*. In this manner, by these three means, God will preserve a remnant of believing Jews and Gentiles alive for the Kingdom to come.

Returning to the *Progression* of the Tribulation, recall the *Pivot Point* prior to the opening of the sixth seal judgment, which we noted was the transition from the Tribulation to the Great Tribulation. It is here we must now address the *Perils* of the Great Tribulation. As the *sixth seal* is broken, the text says,

> **Behold, there was a great earthquake, and the sun became black as sackcloth, the full moon became like blood, and the stars of the sky fell to the earth as the fig tree sheds its winter fruit when shaken by a gale. The sky vanished like a scroll that is being rolled up, and every mountain and island was removed from**

its place. Then the kings of the earth and the great ones and the generals and the rich and the powerful, and everyone, slave and free, hid themselves in the caves and among the rocks of the mountains, calling to the mountains and rocks, "Fall on us and hide us from the face of Him who is seated on the throne, and from the wrath of the Lamb, for the great day of their wrath has come, and who can stand?" (Rev 6:12-17).

The situation has become alarming for all those who reject God, because they know their doom draws nigh.

Then comes the *seventh seal*, and there is a pause, which is the hush of heaven as it anticipates the tremendous final judgments God is about to unleash upon the world. These follow in rapid-fire succession as seven angels blow their trumpets (**Rev 8:1-13; 9:1-21**).

The Trumpet Judgments

The *first trumpet* sounds and brings hail and fire mixed with blood upon the earth, and a third of the earth is burned up (**Rev 8:7**). The *second trumpet* sounds and **"something like a great mountain, burning with fire"** is thrown into the sea, and a third of the sea becomes blood, and a third of things living in the sea die, and a third of the ships are destroyed (**8:8-9**). With the *third trumpet*, a great star falls from heaven to earth, and it contaminates a third of the fresh waters of the earth, and many people die from the poisonous water (**8:10-11**). The *fourth trumpet* sounds and blights a third of the sun and a third of the moon and a third of the stars, so that their light is darkened, and the day/night cycle is disrupted (**8:12**).

At this point, an eagle appears, crying, **"Woe, woe, woe to those who dwell on the earth, at the blasts of the other trumpets that the three angels are about to blow!"** (**Rev 8:13**). The *fifth trumpet* sounds, and the bottomless pit is opened to release hordes of demons who come upon the earth like locusts (**9:1-11**). They will attack those who are not sealed as believers in God, and will inflict such terror and pain that the text says, **"...people will seek death and will not find it. They will long to die, but death will flee from them"** (**9:6**).

Then the *sixth angel* sounds its trumpet, and a great demon army comes numbering two hundred million, killing a third of mankind. Yet remarkably, even in the face of such devastation and terror, those who remain will not repent of their sins and seek the forgiveness of God (**Rev 9:13-21**). Finally, the *seventh angel* sounds its trumpet, and from heaven come loud voices announcing, **"The kingdom of the world has become the Kingdom of our Lord and of His Christ, and He shall reign forever and ever"** (**11:15**). And this seventh trumpet blast ushers in the six rapid-fire *bowl judgments* that are listed in **Revelation 16.**

The Bowl Judgments

The first bowl is poured out on the earth and unloads a *malignant sore* on those people who bear the mark of the beast—the Antichrist—and who worship his image (**Rev 16:2**).[3] The second angel pours its bowl into the sea, and *every living thing in the sea will die* (**16:3**). The third angel then pours out its bowl and all the *fresh water becomes like blood* (**16:4**).

The fourth bowl is then poured out, causing the *sun to scorch men with fire*; in response, they blaspheme the name of God (**16:8**). The fifth angel pours out his bowl on the throne of the beast (another name for Antichrist) and *everything becomes dark*. By this point, those who remain on the earth are said to gnaw their tongues because of pain and sores. But amazingly, despite their sufferings, they do not cease to blaspheme God, nor do they repent of their deeds (**16:10-11**). The sixth angel then pours out his bowl on the great river Euphrates, which—interestingly—is the eastern border of the land promised to Israel (**Gen 15:18; Deut 1:7; Josh 1:4**). With this, *the river's water is dried up*, allowing passage for the kings and their armies arriving from the East, all coming to make war at Armageddon (**Rev 16:12-16**).

Finally, the seventh angel pours out his bowl, and a loud voice from the throne of God announces, **"It is done!"** (**Rev 16:17**). With this judgment comes **"flashes of lightning, rumblings, peals of thunder, and a great earthquake such as there had never**

been since man was on the earth" (**v. 18**). Not only that, great hailstones fall upon the earth, and people curse God because the plague of the hailstones is so severe. This seventh bowl of devastation is the culmination of God's wrath upon the earth. The horrific judgment is concluded. The Purpose, the Prelude, the Pretender, the Progression, the Pivot Point, the Protection, and the Perils of the Tribulation have all been revealed. One feature of the Tribulation remains: its *Promise*.

And what is the *Promise* of the Tribulation? *The Second Coming of Christ,* our topic to consider next.

7

SECOND COMING OF CHRIST

Allusions to the *Second Coming of Christ* permeate both
the Old and New Testaments. In fact, prophecy
accounts for approximately one-fifth of Scripture, and
roughly one-third of those prophecies deal with
Christ's return. All told, there remain over 200
prophecies regarding the return of Christ yet to be
fulfilled. Jesus Himself refers to His return 21 separate
times. One pastor highlights the emphasis of the
Second Coming as depicted in the Bible as follows:

> Prophecy occupies one fifth of Scripture.
> And of that one fifth, one third of that
> focuses on the second coming. There are
> over 650 general prophesies in Scripture, of
> which half of them concern Christ. And out
> of the 330 or so that concern Christ, 225 of
> those point to His second coming. Of the
> forty-six Old Testament prophets, less than
> ten speak of His first coming. Thirty-six

speak of His second coming. There are over 1,500 passages of the Scripture that refer to the second coming, one out of every twenty-five verses in the Bible. For each time the Bible mentions the first coming of the Messiah, it mentions His second coming eight times. For each time the Bible mentions the atonement, it mentions His second coming two times. Jesus referred to His return twenty-one times and over fifty times in the New Testament we are told to be ready for His return.[1]

Over 50 times, He tells His listeners to "Be alert!" or to "Be ready!" Christians need to live in light of Christ's return. As such, we need to know the details of the Second Coming and its practical implications.

Before delving into an overview of the Second Coming, it is important to note some preliminary observations about this event. First of all, as mentioned earlier, the Old Testament believers knew nothing of a "Second" coming of the Messiah even though the Old Testament gave details about the Second Coming. The problem was that the Old Testament Scriptures did not distinguish between the first and second coming with respect to time. The Old Testament saints saw the coming of the Messiah as one event. Many prophetic passages about the two comings combine them or conflate them, so they appear to happen at the same time. The classic example of this is **Isaiah 61:1-3** which describes the coming of the Messiah as one event, yet Jesus made it clear that **verses 1-2a** refer to His first coming in humility and **verses 2b-3** refer to His Second Coming at the end of the age when He comes as the Conquering King. At least 2,000 years transpire between verse 2a and verse 2b. This is typical of prophetic literature in the Bible.

The second truth about the Second Coming is that it is the last great event of world history prior to the recreation of this world for the Millennial Kingdom. Everything that came before was leading up to this amazing climax. And finally, the third basic truth about the Second Coming is that Jesus now comes not to *save* but rather to *judge*. This contrasts greatly with the purpose of His first coming.

This is how Paul describes the Second Coming in **Second Thessalonians 1:7-10**:

> **When the Lord Jesus is revealed from heaven with His mighty angels in flaming fire, inflicting vengeance on those who do not know God and on those who do not obey the gospel of our Lord Jesus. They will suffer the punishment of eternal destruction, away from the presence of the Lord and from the glory of His might, when He comes**

on that day to be glorified in His saints, and to be marveled at among all who have believed, because our testimony to you was believed.

The idea of Christ returning to earth to inflict revenge upon those who reject Him lies in stark contrast to the meekness and gentleness that characterized His first appearance. Regarding Christ's initial coming, Scripture remarks that **"a bruised reed He will not break, and a smoldering wick He will not quench, until He brings justice to victory"** (**Matt 12:20; Isa 42:3**). In **Matthew 11:28-30**, Jesus invites all who are weary and burdened to come to Him, declaring Himself to be (**v. 29**), **"gentle and lowly in heart."** But Christ's second appearance upon the earth promises to be far different from His first. While the Bible tells us Jesus came once in tenderness, it says He will come again in strength and power and might. Whereas He came once as Redeemer, He now comes again as a furious Avenger and a righteous Judge. With His first coming, Jesus came to *save*; at His Second Coming, Jesus comes to *punish*.

And so it is a most unfortunate misconception in the world today that Jesus, even in His anticipated return, remains a perpetually benign, dusty-robed rabbi of docile expression and passive demeanor. That is not at all what the Bible foretells. Rather, it is written of Christ's return that it will kindle such fear in the hearts of the unredeemed that they will cry out to the rocks and mountains to, **"Fall on us and hide us from the face of Him who is seated on the throne, and from the wrath of the Lamb, for the great day of their wrath has come, and who can stand?"** (**Rev 6:16-17**).

In order to encompass all that is written about the Second Coming of Christ, let us consider Christ's return by examining seven of its prominent features: His *Titles*, His *Timing*, His *Train*, His *Tasks*, His *Triumph*, His *Throne*, and His *Tribunal*.

First, what are the *Titles* of the Son of God when He returns? By now, it should be clear that He who returns is the same Jesus Christ of the four Gospels, He who was born to a virgin in Bethlehem, died on a cross at Calvary, was subsequently raised to life and then ascended to heaven. But it is interesting to note that Christ is bestowed with unique titles specifically for this moment of His Second Coming. One of the most descriptive passages portraying the Second Coming of Christ is found in **Revelation 19:11-21**. Here we see Jesus of Nazareth described as a *Rider on a white horse* (**v. 11**). He comes as a warrior, ready to do battle. The same verse says that the One sitting on the horse is called ***"Faithful and True."*** The Lord Jesus is faithful and true in all He does and all He says, including His promise to return and to fulfill all that is promised with His Second Coming. In **verse 12** it says Christ has ***"a name written that no one knows but***

Himself." This is simply a marvelous reminder once again of **Deuteronomy 29:29,** where it declares, **"the secret things belong to the LORD our God."** There are and always will be mysteries about God too wonderful for even God's redeemed to fully comprehend.

Then **verse 13** reveals another name for Christ: *"The Word of God."* This is a remarkable designation, because it illustrates the mysterious and powerful manner by which the witness of Christ is embodied in God's holy Word. This echoes the truth of **Psalm 138:2,** where it says, **"for You** [God] **have exalted above all things Your name and Your word."** God's magnificence is most apparent to us on this earth through His revelation of Himself in His Word (**2 Pet 1:19-21**), and this revelation was exalted to its highest level when His Word became manifest in the form of Jesus Christ—the Word made flesh (**John 1: 1-3, 14; Heb 1:1-3**).

Finally, **verse 16** says, **"On His robe and on His thigh He has a name written,** *King of kings and Lord of lords.***"** Christ comes not only as a Warrior, but also as King, coming to inherit His promised Kingdom and to reign over it.

As to the *Timing* of the Second Coming, there is one main idea to understand: it is a certain event at an uncertain time (cf. **Luke 12:35-40**). Christ's arrival is assured, and will be signaled by certain developments upon the earth, but the *exact time is unknown.* Jesus told

His Apostles in **Matthew 24:36, "But concerning that day and hour no one knows, not even the angels of heaven, nor the Son, but the Father only."** Yet even as Christ tells His followers the exact hour of His return cannot be known, He commands believers to await it expectantly and to know its general *season* by its signs. Jesus repeatedly cautions His followers to watch for His return and to be ready for it (**Matt 24:42,44; Luke 12:40; 21:36**). In another passage, He warns them to **"Stay awake"** (**Mark 13:37**).

Christ even illustrates the importance of vigilant expectation of His return with an illustration from the fig tree (**Matt 24:32-33**). He says: **"From the fig tree learn its lesson: as soon as its branch becomes tender and puts out its leaves, you know that summer is near. So also, when you see all these things** [and by that, He means the events of the Tribulation]**, you know that He is near, at the very gates."** He then tells a parable of ten virgins waiting to meet the bridegroom (i.e. Christ) (**Matt 25:1-13**). Five were wise and took flasks of oil along with their lamps, while five were foolish and brought no extra oil. When the bridegroom was delayed, the foolish virgins— whose oil supply was running low—were obliged to depart in search of more oil for their lamps. When the bridegroom finally came at midnight, the foolish virgins were not present to welcome Him and were shut out of the marriage feast (i.e. Christ's Kingdom).

Jesus finishes the parable by exhorting His listeners to **"Watch, therefore, for you know neither the day nor the hour" (25:13)**.

Elsewhere, the Bible tells us we are to look for (**Phil 3:20; Titus 2:13**), pray for (**Rev 22:20**), and wait for (**1 Cor 1:7; 1 Thess 1:10**) Christ's return. So while it is useless and even foolish to speculate as to the exact hour of Christ's Second Coming, understand that it is equally foolish to fail to note the seasons and events that will herald His return.

What about Christ's *"Train,"* meaning who is coming with Him traveling in His wake? As already noted (**2 Thess 1:7**), Christ will come with His angels (**Matt 25:31**). In **Matthew 16:27**, Jesus declares, **"the Son of Man is going to come with His angels in the glory of His Father...." Mark 8:38** says He will come, **"in the glory of His Father with the holy angels."** So the Lord returns with His angels—that you might expect. But notice who also accompanies Him: *His saints*, those who are His redeemed, His resurrected ones! Do you recall that from the moment of the Rapture on, Christ's followers will always be with Him (**1 Thess 4:17**)? Well, that includes during His glorious return to establish His Kingdom upon the earth! **Zechariah 14:5**, speaking of the day Christ returns, says, **"Then the LORD my God will come, and all the holy ones with Him." Jude 14** says of Christ's return, **"Behold, the Lord comes with ten thousands of His holy ones...."** First

Thessalonians 3:13 exhorts the reader to abound in love, **"so that He may establish your hearts blameless in holiness before our God and Father, at the coming of our Lord Jesus *with all His saints*"** (emphasis added). And notice how Christ's saints are described in **Revelation 19:14**, appearing as **"armies of heaven, arrayed in fine linen, white and pure...following Him on white horses."** Those are Christ's angels and His saints, ready to marvel at His triumphant return.

As to Christ's *Tasks* when He comes, Scripture notes two in particular: He comes to vanquish His opponents, and then to assign them their penalty. In other words, Christ comes first as Conqueror and He comes second as Judge. We might then say within the concept of Christ's *Tasks* in His return are His *Triumph* and His *Tribunal*.

First of all, Christ comes to *Triumph*. And this means He comes to make war against the nations of the earth, those that have rebelled against Him and have followed the Antichrist and his false prophet (**Rev 13:1-18**). What nations are these?

In **Daniel 2** and again in **Daniel 7**, Daniel prophesies four Gentile kingdoms that would successively reign upon the earth: Babylon, Medo-Persia, Greece, and Rome. The times of these Gentile kingdoms began in 605 B.C, when the forces of Babylon, led by Nebuchadnezzar, conquered Jerusalem. Ever since that time, various usurpers in one form or another have presided over Jerusalem and the land promised to Israel. But these days of the Gentiles are about to finally come to an end, just as Jesus has promised (cf. **Luke 21:24**).

The forces that will array themselves against God will represent a reconstitution, or a reconfiguration, of that fourth kingdom, the kingdom of Rome (**Dan 7:24; Rev 17:12**), with the Antichrist at its head. The rebel armies will assemble themselves around Armageddon (**Rev 16:16**), about sixty miles to the north of Jerusalem, but the battle will rage throughout all the land. Here is how God describes Christ's triumphant execution of His enemies at Armageddon: **"So the angel swung his sickle across the earth and gathered the grape harvest of the earth and threw it into the great winepress of the wrath of God. And the winepress was trodden outside the city, and blood flowed from the winepress, as high as a horse's bridle, for 1,600 stadia"** (**Rev 14:19-20**).

As for a more detailed account of the battle, **Revelation 19:11-21** describes it this way: **"Then I saw heaven opened, and behold, a white horse! The one sitting on it is called Faithful and True, and in righteousness He judges and makes war."** Here we see Christ's two tasks: to make war on His enemies and to judge those He subdues. **Verses 12-13** say, **"His eyes are like a flame of fire, and on His head are many diadems, and He has a name written that no one knows but himself. He is** clothed in a robe dipped in blood, and the name by which he is called is The Word of God." This describes Christ's fierce countenance, along with His majestic titles. Not only that, we see Him wearing a robe **"dipped in blood."** The blood is from the war against His enemies as He tramples them underfoot like grapes in **"the winepress of the fierceness and wrath of Almighty God" (19:15).**

Now, **verse 15: "From His mouth comes a sharp sword with which to strike down the nations, and He will rule them with a rod of iron. He will tread the winepress of the fury of the wrath of God the Almighty."** This coincides with the prediction of **2 Thessalonians 1:7-8**, where it speaks of Christ's return in flaming fire, inflicting vengeance upon those who reject Him as their Savior and Lord.

Back to **Revelation 19:17:**

> Then I saw an angel standing in the sun, and with a loud voice he called to all the birds that fly directly overhead, "Come, gather for the great supper of God, to eat the flesh of kings, the flesh of captains, the flesh of mighty men, the flesh of horses and their riders, and the flesh of all men, both free and slave, both small and great."

Zechariah 14 describes this same battle six hundred years before the Apostle John wrote his depiction in the book of Revelation. Zechariah writes that when Christ returns to do battle on that day, His feet will stand upon the Mount of Olives to the east of Jerusalem (**vv. 3-4**). As He touches down, the Mount of Olives will split in two from east to west, creating a wide valley through which waters will flow (**vv. 4, 8**). Zechariah goes on to tell how the enemies of Christ will decompose as they are still standing, so panic-stricken will they be at the spectacle of Christ's return. In fact, the prophet describes how Christ's enemies will actually attack and destroy each other (**vv. 12-13**).

Now, back to Revelation. This is how John concludes his coverage of the battle:

> **And I saw the beast and the kings of the earth with their armies gathered to make war against Him who was sitting on the horse and against His army. And the beast was captured, and with it the false prophet who in its presence had done the signs by which he deceived those who had received the mark of the beast and those who worshiped its image. These two were thrown alive into the lake of fire that burns with sulfur. And the rest were slain by the sword that came from the mouth of Him who was sitting on the horse, and all the**

birds were gorged with their flesh (19:19-21).

So Jesus Christ returns to triumph over His enemies. He decisively overcomes all His opponents. They never had a chance. And once He has triumphed, He is now ready to judge.

Regarding this judgment, it is important to understand where it occurs—at the *Throne* of Christ. **Matthew 25:31** says that, **"When the Son of Man comes in His glory, and all the angels with Him, then He will sit on His glorious throne."** And what is particularly significant about this throne? **"And the Lord God will give to Him the throne of His father David"** **(Luke 1:32)**. Jesus thus inherits and occupies the royal throne of David, in Jerusalem.

From His throne in Jerusalem, Christ Jesus will oversee a *Tribunal*, which He describes in His Olivet Discourse (**Matt 24:3-25:46**). This is sometimes known as the *Judgment of the Nations*, although the verdicts are addressed to individuals and not to nations as a whole. Of note, this trial must be distinguished from the Great White Throne Judgment, which is still to come. In this *Tribunal*, in the time between Christ's Second Coming and His Millennial reign, the survivors of the Great Tribulation and the war at Armageddon come before the Lamb seated upon His throne. Many enemies of Christ will have perished during the Great Tribulation, and many believers will have been martyred (**Rev 6:9-11; 13:7; 17:6**). But there will be survivors as well, including both enemies of Christ and His redeemed, those whom God protected from the perils of the Tribulation.

At this time, those who survived the Tribulation and Second Coming appear before Christ's judgment seat. Jesus says He will place the "sheep"—those who are His redeemed—on His right, and the "goats"—those who rebelled against Him—on His left (**Matt 25:31-46**). To the sheep on His right, He will say, **"Come, you who are blessed by my Father, inherit the Kingdom prepared for you from the foundation of the world"** (**25:34**). The Kingdom inheritance is for those who are blessed by God, those whose deeds give evidence of God's saving grace in their lives (vv. **35-36**). But to the goats on His left He will say, **"Depart from Me, you cursed, into the eternal fire prepared for the devil and his angels"** (**vs. 41**).

Now do you notice something? The eternal fire was prepared for the devil and His demons. It was never the *intention* of God that anyone would join them there. In other words, hell is not made for mankind, and God never predestined any humans to go there. Nevertheless, that is the destiny of all who do not repent and believe in the Son of God—they will die in their sins (cf. **John 8:24**). Those who knowingly and willfully reject Christ face the same fate as Satan himself—eternal damnation in hell, a most frightening prospect. Jesus then concludes His prophecy regarding this future tribunal with these words: **"And these will go away into eternal punishment, but the righteous into eternal life"** (**Matt 25:46**).

8

MILLENNIAL KINGDOM

Here is where we have come so far in our overview of
the order of last things. The *Rapture* will reunite both
the dead and alive of the Church age with Christ. Then
follows the *Tribulation*, when God will pour out His
wrath upon Earth in a series of dreadful judgments.
The Tribulation ends with the *Second Coming* of the
Lord Jesus Christ, when He will triumph over the
forces of evil and will gather all before His throne to
separate the righteous from the unrighteous. This
begins the millennial reign of Christ on the earth.

Let us here make an accounting of those who are
now with Christ. They include His *resurrected Church*,
whose members have all been translated into their
glorified, eternal bodies (**1 Thess 4:17**). They also
include the *Old Testament saints*, whose souls are united
with their eternal resurrection bodies prior to Christ's
Second Coming (**Isa 26:19-20; Dan 12:1-2; John 5:29;
Jude 14; Rev 20:4-6**). All these follow in the wake of

Christ (**Rev 19:14**) as He returns to Earth to meet those of His who survived the Great Tribulation, made up of both Jews and Gentiles. These are the "Tribulation saints," who put their faith in Christ even as the perils of the Tribulation were raging around them. They are still in human form, awaiting entrance into the Millennial Kingdom.

It is toward this last group—the "Tribulation saints"—we now turn our attention, and especially to the Jewish portion of these surviving believers. *This is the long-anticipated remnant of Israel!* These surviving Jewish converts represent the final portion of God's true, covenant people, spoken of from long ago (**Isa 10:20-23**). God protected them during His judgment upon the earth, and now they are situated to inherit the Kingdom promised to them. Of this remnant of Israel, the Apostle Paul writes, **"And in this way all Israel will be saved, as it is written, 'The Deliverer will come from Zion, He will banish ungodliness from Jacob'; 'and this will be My covenant with them when I take away their sins'"** (**Rom 11:26-27**).

This is the New Covenant of blessing being fulfilled from **Jeremiah 31** and **Ezekiel 36**! This is the promise of a new nature washing over this remnant of God's elect! Here we see the fulfillment **Zechariah 12:10** and **Zechariah 13:1**: a chosen remnant of Israel mourning over the Messiah they rejected. When they do, God lets loose a spiritual fountain to cleanse them of their sin and qualify them for His glorious presence.

They are given a new nature of repentance, and their hearts now embrace the Savior their ancestors rejected. With this New Covenant regeneration, these Jewish believers, the prophesied remnant, will enter their promised earthly Kingdom with Christ as their Lord known as the Millennium.

Before surveying the main features of the Kingdom a few notes are in order. The theme of a kingdom on Earth was introduced by God when He created Adam and Eve—He told them to **"rule over the earth"** (**Gen 1:27**). The earthly kingdom promise was formalized with Israel in God's promise to King David (**2 Sam 7:12-13**). Jesus came preaching **"the kingdom of God"** (**Luke 4:43**) and prayed that it would be established on earth (**Matt 6:10**). The Apostle John was given additional information in Revelation developing further, through progressive revelation, God's plan for establishing the fullness of His kingdom on the earth. Revelation unveils the new truth that the kingdom on earth will last for 1,000 years (**Rev 20:1-6**), a truth unknown in the Old Testament and even during Jesus' ministry. "Millennium" is a combination of two Latin words, *mille* meaning "a thousand" plus *annum* meaning "year."

The Redemption of a Sworn Oath
So this is the first item to note about the Millennial Kingdom, Christ's one thousand year reign upon the

earth which follows His return: the *Redemption of a Sworn Oath*—the culmination of God's sworn oath to fulfill His covenant promises.

With the coming of the Millennial Kingdom on the earth, God completes His pact with the nation Israel, fulfilling the oath He swore to her (**2 Sam 7:12-13, 16; Heb 6:13-20**). And what was that oath? The oath of His covenantal promises, which He swore to Abraham and to David, and His promise of New Covenant salvation which He gave to Israel through the prophets Jeremiah and Ezekiel. Do you remember from Chapter 2 how God has promised His chosen people of Israel status as a nation that will bless all other nations, with land having earthly boundaries, and a Kingdom, with a King reigning in Jerusalem? With the coming of the Millennial Kingdom, all these promises are made complete.

This is imperative to understand, because if God does not fulfill His covenantal promises to Israel, then on what basis will He fulfill the promises He makes to those who believe in Him now? In other words, on what grounds can those of the Church be confident God will fulfill His promises to *her* if He will not similarly fulfill all His promises to *Israel*? But God is trustworthy, and He does fulfill *all* His promises—to His Church *and* to Israel (**Ezek 36:22**). **Romans 11:29** declares, **"the gifts and the calling of God are irrevocable." First Samuel 12:22** tells us that God will not forsake His chosen people Israel, because His great name is at stake.

So we see that, just as God foretold, a partial and temporary hardening did come upon Israel following her rejection and crucifixion of the Messiah (**Rom 11:25**). As Paul explains in **Romans 11**, that partial hardening of the heart of Israel allows those who are Gentiles, those who are born outside God's covenantal oaths to Israel, to become children of Abraham by faith (**Gal 3:9, 29**). These Gentile **"children of Abraham by faith"** thus participate in all the earthly and spiritual blessings promised to Israel—*but not to the exclusion of a remnant of ethnic Israel!*

The Removal of the Serpent

This then is the first of *seven features*[1] of the Millennial Kingdom, the *Redemption of a Sworn Oath*. Next God proceeds with the *Removal of the Serpent.* Note John's description in **Revelation 20:1-3**:

> **Then I saw an angel coming down from heaven, holding in his hand the key to the bottomless pit and a great chain. And He seized the dragon, that ancient serpent, who is the devil and Satan, and bound him for a thousand years, and threw him into the pit, and shut it and sealed it over him, so that he might not deceive the nations any longer, until the**

**thousand years were ended. After that
he must be released for a little while.**

At the inauguration of the Millennial Kingdom, God
will capture and incarcerate Satan for a thousand years.
This is a necessary precondition for the Millennial
Kingdom, because if the Kingdom is to be Christ's,
then His great enemy must be removed as a threat (**Ps
110:1; Heb 10:13**). In other words, there can be no
thousand years of peace and righteousness upon earth
if the devil is prowling around seeking whom he might
devour (**1 Pet 5:8**), so God confines him for a time.

But believe it or not, the incarceration of Satan is
not the end of sin upon the earth. And that is because
Satan is not responsible for sin; *the innate sinfulness within
human nature is responsible for sin* (**Rom 3:9; 5:12**). Satan
cannot initiate any sin on his own; he only creates an
environment that predisposes the sinner to sin. So as
we will soon see, although Satan is removed for the
duration of the Millennial Kingdom, sin still percolates
in the hearts of humans.

The Rule of the Son
After the *Redemption of a Sworn Oath* and the *Removal of
the Serpent* comes the *Rule of the Son*. In His Millennial
Kingdom, Jesus will exert undisputed rule over the
entire earth from His throne in Jerusalem,
implementing His rule with a **"rod of iron" (Rev
19:15**), exactly as prophesied in **Psalm 2:9**. Swift and
righteous judgment will proceed from Christ against

any overt rebellion. His rule will be supreme and without challenge.

Why is it imperative for Christ to return in bodily form and rule over the earth? As discussed in the Introduction, all creation has always been under God's sovereign control and subject to His rule. But from the fall of Adam and Eve, it has also been under the sway of sin and under the probationary rule of the devil (cf. **John 14:30; 1 John 5:19**). Since the time of the first transgression, this world has had a usurper presiding instead of its rightful Ruler. But with the coming of the Millennial Kingdom, all that changes. The world gets its rightful Ruler back. Some Christians deny that Jesus will reign on the earth over a physical kingdom. But the Bible clearly teaches that the Messiah will reign literally on the earth (**Ps 2:6-9; 89:20-29**). Zechariah says of the returning Messiah: **"the LORD shall be King over all the earth"** (**14:8**) and His throne will be in **"Jerusalem"** (**v. 4**). He will rule on **"David's throne"** (**2 Sam 7**)—David's throne was on earth, not in heaven. Gabriel reminded Mary of this prophecy, promising her Son would someday assume the rule of David's throne (**Luke 1:32-33**). Luke and Mary, no doubt, understood this prophecy to be fulfilled literally on the earth.

Why must Christ return to rule upon this earth? So that He might have the last word. If the Second Coming merely blended into to the eternal heavenly state, then it could be said that sin had destroyed the world beyond God's ability to repair it. It could be said that God might have won the battle of Armageddon, but the devil would have won the war by accomplishing his purpose—to corrupt beyond repair what God had created.

Accordingly, Jesus must return to a reconstituted earth and rule it as His perfect Kingdom, one in which all the wonders of love, joy, peace, bounty, beauty, harmony, justice, righteousness and goodness prevail. It is only in this way that the Son proves—once and for all—that not only did He conquer sin and death with His triumph at the cross, but with His Second Coming and Millennial rule, He also comprehensively triumphs over all the devil's works. **First John 3:8** says, **"The reason the Son of God appeared was to destroy the works of the devil,"** and with Christ's Millennial rule, this is finally accomplished. By returning to rule on a divinely reconstituted earth, Christ proves that all Satan's schemes ultimately fail to tarnish or stain God's world.

The Resurrection of the Sufferers

We come now to the *Resurrection of the Sufferers*, those who are the Tribulation martyrs. We have already accounted for the arrival of the raptured Church and the Old Testament saints into the Kingdom, following in Christ's train with their resurrected bodies. And we have discussed those believers who survive the Tribulation, the sheep before Christ's throne, who are declared righteous and welcomed into the Kingdom in their as yet-mortal bodies. They are not yet glorified (meaning eternally perfect and immortal), but enter the Kingdom in earthly, "mortal" human form.

One group remains unaccounted for: those who were killed for their faith during the Tribulation, the so-called *Tribulation martyrs*. These are the ones of whom the fifth seal judgment spoke, when their cries for vengeance went up as a prayer to God. They were each given a white robe and told to be patient until the final number of the God's elected martyrs was complete (**Rev 6:9-11**). It is this group that is addressed next in **Revelation 20**, beginning in **verse 4**:

> **Also I saw the souls of those who had been beheaded for the testimony of Jesus and for the Word of God, and those who had not worshiped the beast or its image and had not received its mark on their foreheads or their hands. They came to life and reigned with Christ for a thousand years.**

Thus, the final group of God's redeemed, the Tribulation martyrs, are now resurrected at the outset of the Millennium, so that they also may participate in the reign of Christ upon the earth. With this we see that God forgets none of His own, but keeps His promise to all His chosen ones, a promise of eventual resurrection to life and blessing in His Kingdom (**John**

6:40, 57; 1 Cor 15:22). And don't miss this extraordinary implication: *all* of God's saints therefore share not only in the eternal heavenly Kingdom to come, but also in the Millennial, earthly Kingdom as well! We can now see that the promises God made to His chosen people Israel ultimately extend to everyone who is of God. **Galatians 3:29** proclaims, **"And if you are Christ's, then you are Abraham's offspring, heirs according to promise."** And as **"heirs according to promise,"** all of God's redeemed in Christ partake in the joys and wonders of the earthly Kingdom promised to Israel!

Of course, this was proclaimed in many places throughout the Old Testament, where God promises salvation and Kingdom blessing not only for the people of Israel, but for people everywhere as well. Recall how God told Abraham his Offspring would be a blessing to *all* the nations (**Gen 22:18**). And Isaiah writes of the coming Christ, **"It is too light a thing that you should be My servant to raise up the tribes of Jacob and to bring back the preserved of Israel; I will make you as a light for the nations, that My salvation may reach to the end of the earth"** (**Isa 49:6**). Paul quotes the Old Testament prophet Hosea in **Romans 9:25-26** (quoting from **Hosea 2:23**): **"Those who were not My people I will call 'My people,' and her who was not beloved I will call 'beloved.' And in the very place where it** was said to them, 'You are not My people,' there they will be called 'sons of the living God.'"

In **Romans 15:8-12**, Paul demonstrates the comprehensive manner by which God prophesies Gentile salvation throughout the Old Testament. He cites the Law (**Deut 32:43**), the Prophets (**Isa 11:1; 10**) and the Psalms (**117:1**) to reinforce this point: God had never intended for the Jews to be the end of His blessing. Rather, all along God planned for them to be the means by which He would bring His blessing to the world!

The Reign of the Saints

The *Resurrection of the Sufferers* transitions us now to the *Reign of the Saints*. John writes in **Revelation 20:4: "Then I saw thrones, and seated on them were those to whom authority to judge was committed."** Here we are introduced to the idea of Christ's authority given to His saints to mediate His rule throughout His Kingdom. So who are these saints who will rule in the Millennial Kingdom?

We know this includes the Apostles of Christ. Jesus says in **Matthew 19:28, "'Truly I say to you, in the new world, when the Son of Man will sit on His glorious throne, you who have followed Me will also sit on twelve thrones, judging the twelve tribes of Israel.'"** But these enthroned rulers include more than just the Apostles. In **Revelation 2:26** Jesus says, **"The one who conquers and who keeps My**

works until the end, to him I will give authority over the nations, and he will rule them with a rod of iron, as when earthen pots are broken in pieces, even as I Myself have received authority from My Father." So not only the Apostles, but *all* Christ's resurrected saints (i.e. Church Age, Old Testament, Tribulation martyrs)—now in their glorified, eternal bodies—will rule over the earth with Him. They will mediate God's rule with perfect judgment, because their authority will derive from the Son, who in turn receives His authority from the Father (**Matt 11:27; 28:18; John 4:34**).

The concept of perfect rule over all the earth is utterly foreign in today's world, because all levels of authority in the world today are corrupted by the sinfulness of humans. Thus, we have come to expect imperfect rulers administering imperfect rules with imperfect effect. But that will not be the case in the Millennial Kingdom. Instead, all authority will be just and righteous and true. Christ's resurrected saints will administer perfect rule in His service over the entire earth. It is with this in mind that Paul rebukes the Corinthian church for their trivial grievances against each other. He tells them to forget their petty concerns, reminding them, **"Do you not know that the saints will judge the world?"** (**1 Cor 6:2**).

At this point, one might wonder about the characteristics of the Millennial Kingdom, over which the resurrected saints will rule. In other words, what will the Kingdom be like?[2]

(1) Politically, Israel will be restored to the land promised to Abraham, and it will be the nation that leads the world. Christ will sit upon the throne of David in the restored city of David, Jerusalem. From there, Christ will rule universally, with His saints who will sit with Him on His throne (**Rev 3:21**), functioning as His co-regents, **"and they will reign upon the earth" (Rev 5:10)**. This fulfills the prophecy made by Daniel: **"Then the sovereignty, the dominion and the greatness of all the kingdoms under the whole heaven will be given to the people of the saints of the Highest One"** (**7:27**). And as noted above, Christ's rule will be absolutely righteous, just and true.

(2) Spiritually, all Israel will be converted and will worship Christ the Lamb. And not only Israel but *all* those who enter the Millennial Kingdom, Jew and Gentile alike, will be redeemed followers of Christ. Thus, all who enter the Millennial Kingdom will glorify Christ upon His throne. There will be no false religion, because Satan, the source of all falsehood (**John 8:44**), will have been removed.

(3) Physically, God's curse upon the earth will be lifted. The desert will blossom like a rose (**Isa 35:1**). Streams will run into the desert (**Ps 107:35; Isa 41:18**). A whole valley will open up in the land of Israel and fill with water (**Joel 3:18**). Food will be in abundance

(Joel 2:24), and no one will go without. There will be health and healing and long life (Isa 65:19-20).

In short, Earth will be restored to a sort of pre-Fall, Eden-like state. As it was prior to the entrance of sin, there will no longer be any predation—**"the wolf shall dwell with the lamb, and the leopard shall lie down with the young goat"** (Isa 11:6). Natural disasters will be a thing of the past—no more earthquakes, no more tornadoes, no more hurricanes, no more fear of unforeseen tragedy. The world has been longing for such restoration for ages (Rom 8:20-22), and the Word of God assures that it is coming.

But this time of restoration upon the earth will not occur until all the antecedent events in the *ordo eschaton* have come to pass. That is to say, humans are not now partnering with God to bring about some form of gathering perfection, ultimately culminating in Christ's return and Kingdom fulfillment. Conditions are *not* going from good to better to perfect, as postmillennial adherents would believe. Not only does such thinking strain credulity in the face of the mounting dissipation of humanity, but more importantly it contradicts what the Bible says about the last days (2 Tim 3:1-5).

So when you hear of those who aspire to "partner" with God in bringing Kingdom perfection, ask yourself this: Who cursed the earth in the beginning (Gen 3:17-19; 5:29)? And Who brings destruction upon the earth in the end (2 Pet 3:10)?

The Bible assures us that nothing happens to this earth outside the providential, sovereign determination of God. Thus, God has no partner in bringing Kingdom fulfillment (**Acts 17:25**). He alone will establish His Kingdom when He sends His Son as King, and this will happen only after His judgment has fallen upon the earth.

The Return of Satan

At the close of one thousand years, into this bliss of earthly perfection, comes the *Return of Satan*. **Revelation 20:7-8** reads: **"And when the thousand years are ended, Satan will be released from his prison and will come out to deceive the nations that are at the four corners of the earth...."** This follows John's earlier pronouncement in **Revelation 20:3**, that after the thousand years, Satan **"must be released for a little while."**

Why? Once he's been incarcerated and sequestered for the duration of the Millennial Kingdom, why must Satan now be released back to earth? Answer: because God must confront the remaining covert opposition to the Lord Jesus Christ. You will remember at the advent of the Millennial Kingdom, the only mortals to enter Kingdom are Christ's "sheep," those true believers who survive the Tribulation. But it is important to note that just because they are believers does not mean they have shed their sin nature. Recall that all who follow in

Adam's line are stained by sin (**Rom 5:12**), and this even includes those who are welcomed by Christ into His perfect Kingdom. As these believers enter into and begin to populate the Millennial Kingdom, their sin nature is propagated to succeeding generations as well. Thus, while all those who enter the Kingdom will be true believers, regrettably not all of their offspring will believe. In fact, by the end of the thousand years, John writes that there will be an enormous number of unbelievers, all living in covert rebellion against God (**Rev 20: 8-9**; see below).

Outwardly these unbelievers will be forced to conform to Christ's rule during His reign. As we have already noted, overt expressions of rebellion against His rule will be quashed immediately (**Ps 2:9; Rev 2:27; 19:15**). But *inwardly,* these rebels will harbor sin in their hearts. They will reject Christ and resent His rule. Thus, when Satan is loosed after a thousand years, these rebels are all too willing to come under his aegis, little knowing that all who comprise this latent opposition will soon be destroyed. This is simply further proof of the innate corruption within the heart of mankind. Jesus says, **"And this is the judgment: the light has come into the world, and people loved the darkness rather than the light because their works were evil"** (**John 3:19**). Here you have in the Millennial Kingdom the earth the way it was made to be, with Light of the World (**John 1:9; 8:12**) reigning in Jerusalem. And people will rebel.

The Revolt of Society

So Satan's return leads, lastly, to the final *Revolt of Society*. **Revelation 20:8** says that Satan will **"come out to deceive the nations that are at the four corners of the earth, Gog and Magog, to gather them for battle; their number is like the sand of the sea."** Note that last description. It says the number of rebels **"is like the sand of the sea"** (**20:8**). This reality was noted above: by the end of the millennium, this dormant rebellion will swell to involve many of those on the earth at the close of Christ's Millennial reign. All these will come under the deception and control of Satan as he gathers them to battle against the forces of God.

Continuing at **Revelation 20:9**: **"And they marched up over the broad plain of the earth and surrounded the camp of the saint and the beloved city."** Here we see Satan's forces, arrayed for battle around Jerusalem. And what happens? The text reads, **"...but fire came down from heaven and consumed them, and the devil who had deceived them was thrown into the lake of fire and sulfur where the beast and the false prophet were, and they will be tormented day and night forever and ever"** (**vv. 9-10**).

That is the end of Satan. That is the end of all blasphemy, all disobedience, all sin, all evil. From that point on, all that will ever be known is goodness and righteousness forever. And would you notice something interesting about the fire that comes down out of heaven? This fire is of a cataclysmic sort. **Second Peter 3:10 says, "the heavens will pass away with a roar, and the heavenly bodies will be burned up and dissolved, and the earth and the works that are done on it will be exposed."** This fire will be like an atomic disintegration, engulfing all that was ever created. All animals, birds, fish, plants, oceans, lakes, rivers, mountains, and valleys of the earth—along with all the planets and stars and heavenly bodies throughout the universe—will be consumed in this event.

Two important groups must be considered with regard to this wholesale annihilation. God protects the first group, those who are true believers living upon the earth at the close of the Millennial Kingdom. These He gathers to Himself, resurrecting them to their eternal heavenly form to join the other saints in heaven (**Rev 20:5**). But God vanquishes the second group, the many unbelievers who join Satan's assault upon Jerusalem. Their earthly tenure is over; their eternal doom remains to be enacted.

9

GREAT WHITE THRONE OF JUDGMENT

We now come to the fifth event of the last things, the *Great White Throne Judgment*. With the cataclysmic end of the universe, we find ourselves at **Revelation 20:11-14**. It reads:

> Then I saw a great white throne and Him who was seated on it. From His presence earth and sky fled away, and no place was found for them. And I saw the dead, great and small, standing before the throne, and books were opened. Then another book was opened, which is the book of life. And the dead were judged by what was written in the books, according to what they had done. And the sea gave up the

dead who were in it, Death and Hades gave up the dead who were in them, and they were judged, each one of them, according to what they had done. Then Death and Hades were thrown into the lake of fire. This is the second death, the lake of fire. And if anyone's name was not found written in the book of life, he was thrown into the lake of fire.

So we see the complete disappearance of the world— the entire created universe goes out of existence. Nothing can be seen except a **"great white throne,"** with God seated upon it. And standing before it are all the unredeemed sinners from every time and place since the dawn of creation, now resurrected to their eternal bodies. As to the identity of the Judge upon the throne, the Bible teaches that God the Father, with the Son, judges humanity. Jesus said, **"It is not I alone who judge, but I and the Father"** (**John 8:16**). Jesus sits with His Father on the Father's throne (**Rev 3:21**).

Here you might recall from Chapter 5 that even the unsaved are eventually resurrected. Scripture actually presents two distinct resurrections. All the saints throughout the ages (i.e. Old Testament, Church, Tribulation, Millennial) take part in what is known as the **"resurrection of the just"** (**Luke 14:14**) or the **"resurrection of life"** (**John 5:29**). John refers to it as the **"first resurrection,"** saying, **"Blessed and** holy is the one who shares in the first resurrection! Over such the second death has no power, but they will be priests of God and of Christ, and they will reign with Him for a thousand years" (Rev 20:6).

Then there is the "second resurrection," known as the **"resurrection of judgment" (John 5:29; Dan 12:2)**. This is the resurrection of unbelievers which John includes in **Revelation 20:5**, the dead who **"come to life** [when] **the thousand years** [are] **ended."** Jesus reveals to John that all the unsaved dead from throughout the course of human history are now resurrected. This includes both the **"great and small"** (**Rev 20:12**), meaning those whom the world considered significant and those whose lives seemed inconsequential. They now all stand before God, seated upon His Great White Throne. And books are opened, including the **"book of life"** (**Rev 20:12**), which records the names of all who belong to God by faith (**Dan 12:1; Luke 10:20; Rev 3:5**).

But sadly, none of those now standing before God at His Great White Throne are listed in the **"book of life."** Then God looks at the other books before Him, which are a complete record of every thought, word and deed of all the unrighteous throughout all time, with judgment to be administered based upon the merit of the deeds recorded (**Rev 20:13; Luke 12:47-48**). And here is the horrifying situation: since no thought, word or deed can ever merit God's favor apart from salvation through repentance and faith in His Son, no one standing before God will be exonerated. Each person before the Great White Throne finds that his or her "good" deeds, no matter how beneficent and plentiful, bring only condemnation. Why? Because none of those standing before the throne have imputed to them the righteousness of Christ (**Isa 61:10**; **2 Cor 5:21; Phil 3:9**), spoken of by Jesus as the "wedding attire" mandated for eternal life with God (**Matt 22:1-14**). Without this, God's judgment of **Romans 3:20** pertains: **"For by the works of the law no human being will be justified in His sight"** (Gal 3:11).

Then comes the final verdict in **Revelation 20:14-15**: **"Then Death and Hades were thrown into the lake of fire. This is the second death, the lake of fire. And if anyone's name was not found written in the book of life, he was thrown into the lake of fire."** The "first death" for unbelievers consigns them to hell, to wait for their resurrection at the conclusion of the Millennium Kingdom. The **"second death"** is now upon them, an eternity spent in the **"lake of fire."** This is the most alarming and dreadful passage in the entire Bible. This is the destiny of all who reject Christ and the salvation from sin that He brings through repentance and faith in His substitutionary atonement.

But even in the face of such frightful warning of what is to come, there is still time to avert such a sentence. No one alive today need be consigned to such doom. There is still time to awaken to the truth of God's gospel, to the redemption God has provided through His Son. The prophet Isaiah writes, **"Seek the LORD while He may be found; call upon Him while He is near; let the wicked forsake his way, and the unrighteous man his thoughts; let him return to the LORD, that He may have compassion on him, and to our God, for He will abundantly pardon"** (Isa 55:6-7). And in the New Testament, the Apostle Paul earnestly pleads to those still living under the threat of coming judgment that **"now is the day of salvation"** (**2 Cor 6:2**; **Prov 1:20-23; Heb 3:7-8; 4:7**).

Jesus says, **"Truly, truly I say to you, whoever hears My Word and believes Him who sent Me has eternal life. He does not come into judgment, but has passed from death to life"** (**John 5:24**). That is God's promise to all: if you embrace Christ through repentance, receiving His forgiveness and surrendering to His lordship, you will never be condemned, but inherit eternal life (cf. **John 3:16-18**).

There remains one more event in our series of last things: the New Heaven and New Earth. This is the glorious, eternal dwelling place of God with His angels and His redeemed saints, to which we look in our final chapter.

10

NEW HEAVEN AND NEW EARTH

This brings us, at long last, to the end. Heaven and earth have passed away. All creation has gone from existence. Death and Hades and Satan have been thrown into the Lake of Fire, along with all the unredeemed who have ever lived. Evil has been permanently vanquished.

And so we arrive at the final event in the order of last things, the *New Heaven and New Earth*. This is God's great and glorious grand finale, which is detailed for us in **Revelation 21** and **22**. It is here that we receive a glimpse of heaven as it will be for believers for all time. John writes,

> Then I saw a new heaven and a new earth, for the first heaven and the first earth had passed away, and the sea was

no more. And I saw the holy city, New Jerusalem, coming down out of heaven from God, prepared as a bride adorned for her husband. And I heard a loud voice from the throne saying, 'Behold, the dwelling place of God is with man. He will dwell with them, and they will be His people, and God Himself will be with them as their God. He will wipe away every tear from their eyes, and death shall be no more, neither shall there be mourning, nor crying, nor pain anymore, for the former things have passed away.' And He who was seated on the throne said, "Behold, I am making all things new." Also He said, 'Write this down, for these words are trustworthy and true' (Rev 21:1-5).

What do these six verses show us about the New Heaven and New Earth? Here we see five of its features:

1) a new *Creation by God;*
2) a new *Capital for God;*
3) a new *Connection with God;*
4) a new *Condition of God's elect,* and
5) a new *Confidence in God.*

A New Creation

First, there is a new *Creation by God.* John writes, **"Then I saw a new heaven and a new earth, for the first heaven and the first earth had passed away, and the sea was no more" (Rev 21:1).** This verse establishes, beyond any doubt, that the earth upon which we now exist is temporary. It has always been a *disposable* world to God, part of a disposable universe. It will not survive in its present form. God has established His intent to remake the heavens and the earth. This is not to say that we should be indiscriminate in how we care for the present earth's resources. As in all things delegated to us by God, it should be our intent to be good stewards of the earth for the time it is entrusted to us. We are to care for it and to use it well.

But the idea of *preserving* this world in its present form is futile and runs contrary to the plan of God. The Bible presents a world which is unraveling, on the wane and winding down, because God cursed it when Adam and Eve sinned (**Gen 5:29**). Since that time all creation is **"groaning"** as it undergoes de-evolution and deterioration from the divine curse of the Creator (**Rom 8:18-22**). The processes God has in place are manifestly and unalterably leading to increasing disorder as Earth heads toward extinction. Jesus' implication is undeniable when He claims in **Luke 21:33** that **"'Heaven and earth will pass away....'"** And when He who made the world and holds it together every moment of its existence (**Col 1:17; Heb 1:3**) makes such an assertion, you can bet on it. Thus, the ambitions of those who seek to save the earth in its present form are ultimately at odds with the determinations of God about its destiny, and their attempts to rescue it from certain extinction are a fool's errand. So be comforted—the world's ecological future is not in the hands of humanity; it is headed to a divinely ordained and divinely directed end.

But this does beg the question: why does the universe have to be destroyed and then remade? Why go to all that trouble? Why doesn't God simply remodel the present one?

The answer? *Because the present one is corrupted by sin.*

The universe is not pure in God's sight, and since God ultimately cannot abide *any* impurity (cf. **Ps 24:4; Hab 1:13**), it must be dissolved and remade. **Job 15:15** declares, **"Behold…the heavens are not pure in His** [God's] **sight." Isaiah 24:5** reads: **"The earth lies defiled under its inhabitants, for they have transgressed the laws…."** Therefore, **Psalm 102:25-26** pronounces the consequence of such defilement: **"Of old You laid the foundation of the earth, and the heavens are the work of Your hands. They will perish, but You will remain; they will all wear out like a garment. You will change them like a robe, and they will pass away"**.

A New Capital

Second, we see a new *Capital for God.* This is the **"new Jerusalem,"** which John describes descending (**v. 2**) **"out of heaven from God, prepared as a bride adorned for her husband."** This is the place that Abraham longed to see (**Heb 11:10**), the eternal city that was promised to come (**13:14**). This New Jerusalem becomes the capital city of God's new creation. It is seen coming down from heaven, which means that the city existed prior to its descent. In fact, this is the place Jesus promised to go and prepare for His own (**John 14:1-3**), where deceased saints reside with Him from the time of their departure from the earth until their return in Christ's glorious train at His Second Coming.

This eternal city now descends from its place on high into the New Heavens and New Earth. The metaphor used is of a bride coming to meet her husband (**Matt 25:1-13; Eph 5:25-27**). All the redeemed saints of all time are now with God in the New Jerusalem (**Heb 12:23**), and these saints compose the redeemed Bride promised to Christ by His Father before time began (**John 6:37, 39; Titus 1:2; 2 Tim 1:9**). God now delivers the New Jerusalem with all its saints down to His New Heaven and New Earth as a Bride for His Son, the beloved Bridegroom. And the New Jerusalem becomes the dwelling place of God, His new capital. The text reads, **"And I heard a loud voice from the throne saying, 'Behold, the** dwelling place of God is with man. He will dwell with them, and they will be His people, and God Himself will be with them as their God'" (**Rev 21:3**).

A New Connection

And so we see the third feature of the New Heaven and New Earth: a *New Connection with God*. In their present form on this earth, believers have fellowship with God the Father and with His Son (**1 John 1:3**). Not only do they have Christ's abiding presence at all times (**2 Cor 13:5; Col 1:27**), but also the Father is residing within them as well (**John 14:23**). Not only that, they have God's indwelling Spirit (**Rom 8:11**), sanctifying them moment by moment as He guides their thoughts, words, and deeds. In other words, the entire Trinity is present within the redeemed of God living upon the earth! In fact, that is the easiest, clearest way to understand the difference between a Christian and a non-Christian: a Christian is *someone in whom God lives*.

But believers in this world have a finite, carnal form that does not allow them to behold God as He truly is. They do not get to see God in the fullness of His glory...*yet*. In **Exodus 33:20,** God says to Moses, **"You cannot see My face, for man shall not see Me and live"** (Judges 13:22). In **1 Timothy 6:16,** Paul reasserts that God **"alone has immortality, who dwells in unapproachable light, whom no one has**

ever seen or can see." The present mortality of all humans limits their experience of the wonders of God. However, all that changes in the New Heaven and New Earth. In that time, in their glorified form, believers will *see the glory of God* (**Matt 5:8; 1 Cor 13:12**). God will finally dwell with His people in fullness, which has always been His intent (**Ezek 37:27; Rev 21:3**). This is the ultimate fulfillment of God's name, **"Emmanuel"** which means **"God with us"** (**Isa 7:14**).

How can this be? It is because believers will have exchanged their finite, sinful, fleshly bodies for eternal, holy, spiritual ones. Then, the new eternal nature *already given to believers here on earth* will be matched with a perfected body incapable of transgression. In this new, eternal, glorified state to come, believers will be free of sin. In fact, the Bible says redeemed believers in glory will be forever unable to sin (**Rom 8:20-21; 2 Pet 1:4**)! They will be forever pure, just as Jesus is pure (**1 John 3:2**).

Well, Jesus gave a statement about purity in **Matthew 5:8**. Do you recall this Beatitude? He said, **"Blessed are the pure in heart, for they will see God."** Those who are pure in heart will, for the first time, actually *see God's glory*. On this earth, believers never attain purity. They are to strive for it, but it eludes them as a result of their innate sinfulness (**Rom 7:17-19**). But one day, all that will change. Believers will be pure and, as a result, they will see God. This will be a new connection to God, a new experience of God. That promise should get the believer's heart to race and spirit to soar!

And something else in the believer's connection with God will change. In this world, the Bible says the blood of Christ purifies believers so that they are able *to serve God* (**Heb 9:14**). In heaven, too, believers will serve God. It says in **Revelation 7:15** that the saints **"are before the throne of God, and serve Him day and night in His temple."** But do you realize that in the New Heaven and New Earth, not only will believers serve God, *but Christ will serve them*? This is also part of the new Connection with God! Jesus says in **Luke 12:37, "Blessed are those servants whom the Master finds awake when He comes. Truly, I say to you, He will dress Himself for service and have them recline at table, and He will come and *serve them*"** (emphasis added). Such a promise is almost too marvelous to imagine—the Savior of the world, God Himself, serving the sinners He has redeemed!

A New Condition

Fourth, there is a new *Condition of God's elect*. John writes, **"He will wipe away every tear from their eyes, and death shall be no more, neither shall there be mourning, nor crying, nor pain anymore, for the former things have passed away. And He who was seated on the throne said, 'Behold, I am**

making all things new"' (**Rev 21:4-5**). The believer's condition is so wondrously new that John has trouble characterizing it! Notice how John can only describe it negative terms: no more death, no more mourning, no more crying, no more pain. He can only report what he sees by reporting what he doesn't see! The joyful vision that John is given is so new and glorious that there is no apt description for it. John has no words to describe the heavenly state because he is limited to communicate only with that which can be experienced or imagined. In other words, John is saying this New Heaven and New Earth is beyond our experience or imagination—present language cannot do justice in presenting the image.

All things will be brand new for believers: their resurrected bodies (**1 Cor 15:53; 1 John 3:2**), their eternal dwelling place, all that can be experienced— *brand new.* **First Corinthians 15:42-44** says of believers that here they are perishable; there they are imperishable. Here they know dishonor; there they will know glory. Here they know weakness; there they will know power. It will be absolute eternal bliss. Everyone will forever experience unceasing joy in the presence of God—unmitigated, unlimited, undiminished elation, forever and ever.

A New Confidence

Fifth, there is a new *Confidence in God* for believers to have—*now, in the present.* Jesus says, **"Write this down,** for these words are trustworthy and true" **(Rev 21:5)**. This is not to say that some portion of Scripture is not trustworthy and true. All Scripture is "**breathed out by God**" (**2 Tim 3:16**), and what God says is always perfectly trustworthy and always completely true. So we can be assured Jesus is not trying to qualify here what He has just told John as being more trustworthy or truer than other biblical passages. Rather, Jesus is giving all these revelations to John and commanding that he should write them down so that believers can have a *renewed* confidence in Him. As we draw near to the end of His story, Jesus wants to *reinvigorate* the believer's confidence in Him, to assure the believer that He is guiding all things along according to His perfect will and in His perfect power (**Eph 1:11**).

Then He tells John, **"It is done! I am the Alpha and the Omega, the beginning and the end"** (**Rev 21:6**). Jesus uses the first and last letters of the Greek alphabet to describe Himself. By doing so, He establishes that He was there at the beginning, receiving the promise of glory from His Father. And He is there at the end, ensuring the perfect culmination of all things. He uses this moniker to express the extent and finality of all that He has accomplished and all that He has revealed, and to affirm His credentials in telling us what will be.

The Eternal Glory of God

And now comes the end, and it is divinely sublime. This final act in God's Word is provided by Paul in **1 Corinthians 15**. Jesus, the Bridegroom, has assumed rulership over the Kingdom given to Him by His Father. He has received from the Father His Bride of redeemed sinners, prepared for Him from before the foundation of the world (**Eph 1:4; Rev 13:8; 17:8**). Now, in an act of reciprocal love, Jesus returns to His Father the love gift given to Him. Beginning at **verses 24-25**, Paul writes: **"Then comes the end, when He delivers the Kingdom to God the Father after destroying every rule and every authority and power. For He must reign until He has put all His enemies under His feet."** This is what Jesus Christ does in returning to Earth, destroying His enemies and reigning upon David's throne in Jerusalem in the Millennial Kingdom.

Paul then continues: **"The last enemy to be destroyed is death. For God has put all things in subjection under His feet"** (**1 Cor 15:26-27**). This is reminiscent of **Matthew 28:18**, where Jesus says, **"All authority in heaven and earth has been given to Me"** (**John 3:35; 5:22**). And then in **1 Corinthians 15:28** comes a most magnificent promise: **"When all things are subjected to Him** [in other words, to Jesus, the Son of God]**, then the Son Himself will also be subjected to Him** [that is, God the Father]**, that God may be all in all."**

It all started with God desiring that His Son would receive the glory due His name (**John 17:5**). And so the Father set about to redeem a Bride of sinners for His Son, a Bride over which He would rejoice, for this Bride would render perfect praise to the Son throughout eternity (**Isa 62:5**). Now we have arrived at the end, and we see it recapitulates the beginning: Father and Son and Holy Spirit enjoying perfect inter-Trinitarian fellowship. Christ, through His death and resurrection, has received all the glory due His name (**Phil 2:9-11**).

But something has been added to the Trinity in going from the beginning to the end of God's glorious story: *the redeemed Bride of Christ!* All the believers of all time are now there with the Trinity in glory as the Bride of Christ, having been delivered by the Bridegroom back to the Father. Believers are forever, **"set free from...bondage to corruption,"** having obtained **"...the freedom of the glory of the children of God"** (**Rom 8:21**). Believers experience true freedom in being permanently united with the Godhead forevermore! (**John 8:36**). Jesus had prayed to His Father, **"Father, I desire that they also, whom you have given Me, may be with Me where I am, to see My glory that you have given Me because You loved Me before the foundation of the world"** (**John 17:24**). And here, when everything is completed, we find that Jesus' prayer has come true, exactly as He prayed it!

Before time began, God the Father determined to glorify His Son by giving to Him a Bride, who would forever extol Him for His glory. And in **John 17:10**, in prayer to His Father, Jesus encapsulates this final state: **"All mine are yours, and yours are mine, and I am glorified in them."** This is the conclusion toward which all things are inexorably moving. Christ is to be forever glorified with perfect praise from the Bride He has redeemed. This will all come true, just as God purposed from the beginning.

This is the hope of all who believe in Jesus, to be with Him, to see His glory, to eternally praise and glorify God, the Three in One. This is the destiny for all God's redeemed—a state of eternal bliss: eternal joy from an eternal communion with an eternal God.

"He said, 'Go your way, Daniel,
for the words are shut up
and sealed
until the time of the end.'"

Daniel 12:9

NOTES

Introduction

1. Adapted from John MacArthur, from the sermon, "Why Every Calvinist Should Be a Pre-Millennialist, Part 1," Grace Community Church, Sun Valley, CA, March 25, 2007.

2. Is. 61:1, 2; Luke 4:17-22.

3. John MacArthur, from the sermon, "The Coming Kingdom of Christ, Part 3," Grace Community Church, Sun Valley, CA, April 6, 1980.

Chapter 1—Before Time Began

1. This is one of Jesus' favorite references for Himself as seen in the Gospels (Matt 16:27; 19:28; 26:64; Mark 2;10; 8:31; Luke 5:24; John 13:31). When Jesus uses it in reference to Himself, His listeners would have known He was referring directly to this promise from Daniel, and the He was announcing Himself as the singular heir to this remarkable inheritance. In using this term in self-reference, Jesus proclaims Himself to be Messiah and King.

Chapter 2—Israel: Key to the Future

1. William D. Barrick, "The Mosaic Covenant," *TMSJ* 10.2 (Fall, 1999): 213.

2. William D. Barrick, "Inter-covenantal Truth and Relevance: Leviticus 26 and the Biblical Covenants," *TMSJ*, 20.1 (Spring 2010): 81-102.

Chapter 3—Daniel Looks Ahead

1. Isaac Newton, *Observations upon the Prophecies of Daniel, and the Apocalypse of St. John* (J. Darby and T. Browne, 1733).

2. John C. Whitcomb, "Daniel's Great Seventy-Week Prophecy," *GTJ* (Fall 1981): 259.

3. Daniel prophesies in remarkable detail about the reign of Antiochus IV "Epiphanes" (over three-hundred years prior to its fulfillment!) in **Daniel 11:21-35**.

4. See Harold Hoehner, *Chronological Aspects of the Life of Christ* (Grand Rapids: Zondervan) 1977.

5. We explore this time of the Tribulation in Chapter 6.

6. Michael Rydelnik, Daniel, *The Moody Bible Commentary* (Chicago: Moody, 2014), 1306.

Chapter 5—Rapture

1. *Bema* is used in 2 Cor 5:10 and means "a step" or raised platform used in ancient times as a speaker's platform or judicial bench.

Chapter 6—Tribulation

1. John MacArthur, *The MacArthur Study Bible*, 1970.

2. The evangelical witness of the 144,000 during the Tribulation will be aided by two special witnesses, discussed in **Revelation 11**, and by a flying angel witness spoken of in **Revelation 14.**

3. This "mark of the beast" is the well-known symbol "666" (**Rev 13:18**).

Chapter 7—Second Coming of Christ

1. John MacArthur, from the sermon "Worshipping the Worthy Lamb," Grace Community Church, Sun Valley, CA, March 14, 1999.

Chapter 8—Millennial Kingdom

1. This section on seven features of the Millennial Kingdom is adapted from John MacArthur, from the sermon series "The Coming Earthly Kingdom of the Lord Jesus Christ, Parts 1-4," delivered at Grace Community Church, Sun Valley, CA, October 9-November 13, 1994.

2. These descriptions of the political, spiritual, and physical characteristics of the Millennial Kingdom are from John MacArthur, "The Coming Earthly Kingdom of the Lord Jesus Christ, Part 3," Grace Community Church, Sun Valley, CA, November 6, 1994.

ABOUT THE AUTHOR

Colin Eakin is an orthopedic surgeon in Palo Alto, California and a member of Creekside Bible Church (formerly Grace Bible Fellowship, Silicon Valley), where he teaches in various capacities. He is the author of *God's Glorious Story*. He and his wife Michelle live in Menlo Park, California with their children Hunter and Charlotte.

ABOUT GBF PRESS

GBF Press is the book publishing ministry of Grace Bible Fellowship of Silicon Valley. We started this publishing ministry out of the simple desire to serve our local body with substantive biblical resources for the sake of our people's growth and spiritual maturity.

But we also believe that book publishing, like any other Christian ministry, should first and foremost be under the supervision and accountability of the local church. While we are grateful for and will continue to support the many excellent traditional publishers available today–our shelves are full of the books they have produced–we also believe that the best place to develop solid, life-giving theology and biblical instruction is within the local church.

GBF Press is also unique because we offer our books at a very low cost. We strive for excellence in our writing and seek to provide a high-quality product to our readers. Our editorial team is comprised of men and women who are highly trained and excellent in their craft. But since we are able to avoid the high overhead costs that are typically incurred by traditional publishers, we are able to pass significant savings on to you. The result is a growing collection of books that are substantive, readable, and affordable.

In order to best serve various spiritual and theological needs of the body of Christ, we have developed three distinct lines of books. **Big Truth|little books**® provides readers with accessible, manageable works on theology, Christian living, and important church and social issues in a format that is easy to read and easy to finish. Our **Equip Series** is aimed at Christians who desire to delve a little deeper into doctrine and practical matters of the faith. Our **Foundations Series** is our academic line in which we seek to contribute to the contemporary theological discussion by combining pastoral perspective with rigorous scholarship.

OTHER TITLES FROM GBF PRESS

Please visit us at GBFPress.com
to learn more about these titles

BIG TRUTH little books®

What the Bible Says About Gray Areas
Cliff McManis

Faith: The Gift of God
Cliff McManis

How to Pray for Your Pastor
Derek Brown

The Problem of Evil
Cliff McManis

What the Bible Says About Government
Cliff McManis

God Defines and Defends Marriage
Cliff McManis

*Protecting the Flock: The Priority of
Church Membership*
Cliff McManis

What the Bible Says About Confrontation
Cliff McManis

*Fellowship with God: A Guide to Bible Reading,
Meditation, and Prayer*
Derek Brown

Equip
*The Biblically-Driven Church:
How Jesus Builds His Body*
Cliff McManis

*God's Glorious Story:
The Truth of What It's All About*
Colin Eakin

*Strong and Courageous: The Character and Calling of
Mature Manhood*
Derek Brown

*The Gospel, the Church, and Homosexuality: How the
Gospel is Still the Power of God for
Redemption and Transformation*
Edited by Michael Sanelli and Derek Brown

Foundations
Apologetics by the Book
Cliff McManis

Made in the USA
San Bernardino, CA
20 March 2020